# THE EXPERT WITNESS

# ONE WEEK LOAN

# The Expert Witness

## A Practical Guide

Catherine Bond
Mark Solon
Penny Harper
Gill Davies

*Third Edition*

Shaw & Sons

*Published by*
Shaw & Sons Limited
Shaway House
21 Bourne Park
Bourne Road
Crayford
Kent DA1 4BZ


© Shaw & Sons Limited 2007

First published November 1997
Second Edition November 1999
Third Edition November 2007


ISBN 0 978 0 7219 1442 8


A CIP catalogue record for this book is available
from the British Library

*Printed in Great Britain by*
Athenæum Press Limited, Gateshead

# SUMMARY OF CONTENTS

# CONTENTS

*Contents*

# PREFACE

Often expert witnesses start by chance. They are instructed on one case and gradually over time develop an ad hoc system of producing reports and going to court. They hope they will get more work and they hope they are doing things right. Rarely do they get any independent appraisal of their work and they learn as they go along by trial and error.

This is clearly a very unsatisfactory state of affairs for clients, lawyers and the court. It may stem from the fact that experts do not see that they have two roles:

First as a professional in their chosen field. They will have spent many years and a great deal of money gaining the necessary qualifications and experience to have the knowledge to be professional. They participate in continuing education to keep their knowledge up to date so they can follow their profession.

Second as an expert, including as a witness. This is a separate role that has its own disciplines and skills. Expert witnesses need to be able to communicate the hard won knowledge of their professional field in a legal setting. They are unaware of the practices and procedures. Surprisingly and in stark contrast to being trained for the first role, expert witnesses often have no training at all for this second role.

Cases can be won or lost on the strength of expert evidence and clients expect the paid professional witnesses their solicitors use to do their very best.

Many experts Bond Solon have trained requested a straightforward guide on how the legal system works and the expert's part within it. There are many legal textbooks for lawyers but often these are inaccessible to experts. We have tried to make this guide as practical and easy to read as we can but without being simplistic.

The first edition of this book proved to be very popular. This third edition has been updated to reflect on what has happened since the current Civil Procedure Rules came into force. This new edition discusses how the law and procedure are evolving in this area and the impact of these changes on the way the expert carries out his role. It is vital for experts, even experienced ones, to revisit and rethink what they do – by attending training courses and studying the rules and commentaries upon them.

The law is stated as at September 2007 and as it applies to England and Wales. However, many principles apply to all legal jurisdictions, for example the importance of independence and clear communication in particular.

## The Authors

All are solicitors and have been involved in the design, development and delivery of training for expert witnesses. Catherine Bond has worked with Withers and Wilde Sapte in the City and Crowell & Moring in the United States. Gill Davies was head of the Expert Witness Group at Bond Solon and previously worked as a commercial litigator and professional support lawyer at major city firms. Penny Harper has worked with Kingsley Napley and is a Director of Bond Solon. She has particular experience in the design of accredited knowledge and skills training. Mark Solon is also a Director of Bond Solon and has worked with Clyde & Co in the City and had his own practice, Young & Solon for 10 years in London.

## Bond Solon Training

Since 1992, Bond Solon has been the leading provider of training for expert witnesses. Many tens of thousands of experts have taken the programmes offered by Bond Solon and attended the annual expert witness conference. As well as training individual experts, Bond Solon also provides extensive in-house training for specialist groups of experts and offers university certified programmes with Cardiff University Law School.

Bond Solon
13 Britton Street
London
EC1M 5SX

Enquiries to 020 7253 7053
Find out more at www.bondsolon.com

# Chapter 1

# EXPERT EVIDENCE IN CONTEXT

**SUMMARY**

- The English legal system
- Reform of the role of experts in the Civil and Criminal Justice System
- Who is who in the legal system

**The criminal courts**
- Court structure
- The personnel
- The parties
- The burden of proof
- How criminal cases start
- Evidence in criminal trials
- Witnesses in criminal trials
- The role of the expert in a criminal trial
- Procedure of a criminal trial

**The civil courts**
- Court structure
- The personnel
- The civil justice tracking system
- The parties
- The burden of proof
- How civil cases start and proceed
- Evidence in civil trials
- Witnesses in civil trials
- The role of experts and expert reports

# The English Legal System

There are two types of cases within the English legal system. These are **Criminal Cases**, where the state takes action against an individual to determine if that individual is guilty or not guilty of a crime, and **Civil Cases** which involve an individual, business or organisation taking action against another, usually to obtain money. There are accordingly different courts and procedures depending on whether a case is a criminal case or a civil case.

A broad overview of the court system is set out below. In addition, there are also numerous tribunals such as employment tribunals, immigration tribunals and so on.

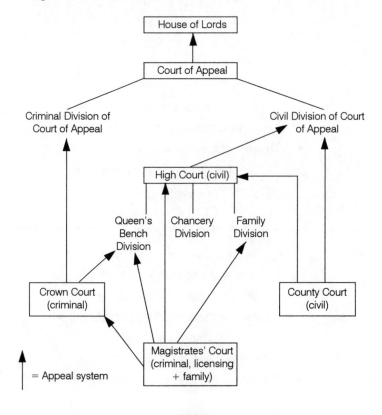

## THE ADVERSARIAL SYSTEM

In both civil and criminal cases in the United Kingdom, there is basically an adversarial system.

Two parties come before the court; their version of events or their views on the law are in dispute. They are usually represented by lawyers who argue or advocate their case. The court must find out what happened, taking into account evidence of facts and sometimes opinion evidence. Facts are what someone saw, heard or did. Opinion evidence is given by expert witnesses. The opinion expressed is an independent view of the facts and issues in dispute which the expert gives to help the court to understand and to decide the case. Experts' qualifications and experience enable them to form such an opinion. For example, a surveyor might say that cracks in a wall did not arise as a result of subsidence.

Each party, usually represented by its lawyers, is entitled to call its own evidence, subject to the control of the court. In civil cases in particular, the court will decide early in each case the evidence it is likely to need, including from witnesses of fact and expert witnesses. Each party also has the opportunity to cross-examine, by means of critical questions, the evidence of its opponent's witnesses. The court will also look at other evidence such as documentary evidence or real evidence, for example the knife used to commit a killing.

The adversarial system represents a debate between the two parties. The lawyers represent their clients and they present arguments about the merits of their side's case. Each side may have its own expert witnesses or, increasingly in civil cases in particular, there may be one single expert jointly instructed by the parties.

It is vital that expert witnesses are independent. They should not simply follow the wishes of the lawyers (or their clients) whose main role is to "win" the case for their client by representing their interests to the best of their ability. The role of experts is that of independent educators; they are there to assist the court to reach a fair decision.

## REFORM OF THE ROLE OF EXPERTS IN THE CIVIL AND CRIMINAL JUSTICE SYSTEM

### Experts appearing in the Civil Courts

The civil courts have moved away from the adversarial system. Reforms over the past 20 years have concentrated on a "cards on the table" approach during litigation: "trials by ambush" have been a thing of the past for some time. Lord Woolf's Access to Justice reforms, culminating in the Civil Procedures Rules (1998) and introduced in the courts in April 1999, went much further. They encouraged parties and their lawyers to:

- View litigation as a last resort and to try to settle the dispute quickly by negotiation or other means to save time and costs and to reduce the stress factor.

- Co-operate with the other party by sharing information and even experts.

The Civil Procedure Rules (1998) also:

- Provide *one* set of more user-friendly plain English rules for all the civil courts instead of different rules for the different courts.

- Give the judges in the civil courts much wider powers than before to control how cases are run – no longer do they have to wait for a party to "make an application" but they can act on their own initiative, including to:

  — throw out one party's case completely;

— control the amount of work, time and legal costs put into a case, especially by a "richer" party to try to ensure it is "proportionate" to what is in dispute;

— curtail the evidence which a party can use; and

— limit the length of a trial.

The system remains basically adversarial but the judges have quasi inquisitorial powers.

- Emphasise the client's role in the key decisions in the action: the client, rather than the lawyer should usually sign the new style "pleadings"; it is the client who has to search for the necessary documents to be disclosed to the other party and explain how he has done this; and the court can require the client, not just the lawyer, to attend court for any hearing.

In the new style civil litigation, some of the power to run and manage a case has been transferred from the lawyers to the court.

All experts who practise in the civil courts need to study the new rules and procedures carefully. The most relevant part of the rules and practice directions, Part 35, which deals specifically with expert evidence, is at Appendix 4. The role and function of experts is *very different* under this procedure and the more important aspects are referred to throughout the text. However, experts should also look carefully at the following Parts of the Civil Procedure Rules 1998:

- Part 1 – the Overriding Objective: a set of guiding principles to underpin the rules.

- Part 3 – the Court's Case Management powers.

- Parts 26-29 – which cover in more detail how different types and sizes of cases will be managed and organised in future.

## Experts appearing in the Criminal Courts

There have been several reviews over the last decade which are starting to have an impact on expert evidence in the criminal justice system. Part 33 of the Criminal Procedure Rules (CrPR) came into effect in 2006: it contains very similar provisions to Part 35. Part 33 of the Criminal Procedure Rules (CrPR) deals with criminal expert evidence and is at Appendix 6. In particular, it states that an expert's duty is to the court and that expert evidence can only be adduced if the experts have engaged in a pre-hearing discussion and if more than one party wishes to introduce expert evidence. If only one party wishes to use expert evidence, they must inform the other party.

In February 2006, the Crown Prosecution Service published Annex K to its Disclosure Manual. Prosecution expert witnesses will be required to follow the guidelines set out in the Annex entitled "Disclosure: Experts' Evidence and Unused Material – Guidance Booklet for Experts".

Further, in *R v Harris* [2005] EWCA Crim 1980 and *R v Bowman* [2006] EWCA Crim 417, the Court of Appeal have taken guidance from a civil case (*Ikarian Reefer* [1993] 2 Lloyd's Rep 68) and from the CPR and sought to impose the same duties on experts instructed by the prosecution and the defence as are imposed on civil expert witnesses. These cases preceded the introduction of the CrPR Part 33, which has codified these principles.

## Experts appearing in the Family Courts

The Family Courts are moving towards a similar position to those in the civil and criminal courts. The Family Procedure Rule Committee is currently working on a draft practice direction relating to the use of experts in family proceedings. This is likely to follow a similar format to the rules in the civil and criminal courts.

Already in adoption proceedings, there are very similar provisions operating to CPR Part 35 and CrPR Part 33. Part 17 of the Adoption

Rules is supplemented by a Practice Direction which sets out in detail what an expert's report for use in adoption proceedings should contain.

## THE LEGAL PROFESSION – WHO'S WHO?

### Solicitors

Solicitors form partnerships or work as sole traders to provide legal services, from offices. They are available to give advice directly to members of the public and to businesses and organisations. The professional body for solicitors is the Law Society.

Solicitors are responsible for the whole case management, for example advising the client, arranging meetings with barristers, preparing documents for court and negotiating settlement of the case. Thus the day-to-day running of the case is done by solicitors. It is the solicitors who instruct experts.

Solicitors have rights of audience in the Magistrates' Court, the County Court and sometimes in the Crown Court and High Court.

### Barrister/Counsel

Barristers work on an individual self-employed basis. Generally, members of the public cannot go directly to barristers for advice (direct instructions to barristers are allowed from some professionals, e.g. surveyors, and from some organisations, e.g. Citizens Advice Bureaux). Barristers are instructed by solicitors and sometimes other professions to give advice on points of law and procedures and to represent members of the public in court. The solicitors send barristers documents which summarise what it is that the solicitor wants the barrister to do; these documents are called briefs. Barristers have rights of audience, meaning they can represent a client, in all the courts. They share offices called "chambers" with other barristers.

## Conferences

"Conference with counsel" is a meeting in which barristers or solicitor advocates give advice. The instructing solicitors and their clients, and sometimes the experts, attend such conferences. Experts can use these meetings to help counsel to understand the issues and see the strengths and weaknesses highlighted by the expert opinion.

## QCs/Silks/Leading Counsel

A QC is a senior barrister with usually at least 20 years' experience or "call" as a barrister. Junior Counsel is a barrister of any number of years' experience, who has not become a QC. In many cases it will only be necessary to have one barrister, a Junior Counsel or a solicitor with the appropriate advocacy experience.

The old system for the appointment of QCs, which was based on taking "soundings" from other members of the legal profession, has been replaced and the first QCs to be appointed under the new system were announced in 2006.

## Training of Solicitors and Barristers

Both solicitors and barristers study law degrees or do a non-law degree followed by an intensive year of legal studies for the Common Professional Exam (CPE). After this they make a personal choice as to whether they want to be solicitors or barristers. Those who want to become solicitors take a further one year's study with exams, called the Legal Practice Course (LPC); they must then do two years in a solicitors' firm in a training contract before they qualify as solicitors. Those who want to become barristers do one year's study on a Bar Vocational Course with exams. When they have passed these exams, they can then call themselves barristers. However, to practise as a self-employed barrister they must undertake one year's pupillage, where they learn from a senior barrister. Solicitors who wish to practise advocacy in the higher courts need to qualify for this additional role through demonstrating appropriate experience or by training, assessment and examination.

## Legal Executives and Paralegals

Legal executives and paralegals are sometimes employed in solicitors firms to do some of the more routine work. They may not have degrees; they may start work with a law firm after leaving school and learn on the job. Others will have degrees and work in a firm before undertaking or completing their training to become a solicitor. Legal executives also take some exams in law with the Institute of Legal Executives (ILEX). Fellows of the Institute have similar rights to practise in the courts as solicitors.

## The Crown Prosecution Service (CPS)

This is staffed by lawyers who are paid by the state to prosecute criminal cases. In Magistrates' Courts lawyers working for the CPS usually represent the prosecution. However, they do not yet have the right to appear in the Crown Court. This means that, in the Crown Court, the prosecution will always be represented by a barrister instructed by the CPS.

## Judges

There are many different sorts of judges. They are independent and listen to both parties in any dispute before making a decision to resolve it. The Judicial Appointments Commission selects candidates for appointment to judicial offices after a competitive process. The Lord Chancellor is responsible for making the appointments and recommending those selected by the JAC to the Queen. Judges are employed by the State.

District judges, who often previously worked as solicitors, manage the pre-trial work of most claims in the County Court and hear the trials of cases up to £15,000. Circuit judges hear the larger County Court civil claims and most criminal trials. High Court judges, assisted by Masters, hear cases both civil and criminal in the High Court.

# The Criminal Courts

The vast majority of criminal cases are brought against a defendant by the State, although occasionally there are private prosecutions. The Crown Prosecution Service (CPS) is usually responsible for the prosecution of the defendant.

## COURT STRUCTURE

### Magistrates' Court

All criminal cases have initial proceedings in the Magistrates' Court and over 90% are completed there. The magistrates will decide whether a defendant is to be held in custody to await trial – the court hearing – at which it will be decided if the defendant is guilty or not guilty, or whether the defendant will be granted bail and released on the condition that they return to court on a particular date. They also decide if a defendant is entitled to legal aid. Finally they may have to decide whether the defendant's trial will take place in the Magistrates' Court or in the Crown Court (see flow diagram on page 16).

Criminal trials that take place in the Magistrates' Court are called **summary trials**. Summary trials are used to try the less serious crimes, for example minor road traffic offences such as speeding, driving without a licence or careless driving; cases of shoplifting, theft of small amounts, minor offences against the person or against property are also commonly dealt with by summary trial. 95% of criminal trials are summary trials.

A summary trial will be heard by the magistrates who will decide if the defendant is guilty or not guilty. A psychologist may be involved in giving expert opinion on whether a defendant is fit to give evidence at trial. The magistrates will also pass sentence but, in some cases, they can send the defendant to Crown Court for sentencing if they consider their own powers of sentencing are inadequate and a higher penalty is required. They will often adjourn to get pre-sentence reports by the Probation Service before passing sentence. An expert, for example a psychiatrist, may be involved in helping to prepare a pre-sentence report. This report is used to help decide which sentence is most suitable.

### Who Sits (Makes the Decision)

There will usually be three lay magistrates on the "bench". These will be three non-lawyers who have volunteered to sit as Justices of the Peace. They will be assisted in matters of law and practice by a legally qualified Magistrate's Clerk. Sometimes, instead of three lay magistrates there will be one stipendiary magistrate sitting alone. The stipendiary magistrate will be a qualified barrister or solicitor with at least seven years' experience.

### Correct Form of Address

Magistrates should be addressed as "Sir" or "Madam".

## The Crown Court

The Crown Court tries the more serious crimes. Trial in the Crown Court is known as trial on **indictment**. The indictment sets out the charges against the defendant. The sorts of case that will be heard in the Crown Court are murder, rape, fraud, drug offences, robbery, burglary, serious offences against persons and property, dangerous driving.

The Crown Court also hears appeals from the Magistrates' Court and cases in which the magistrates have committed the defendant for sentence.

### Who Sits

Crown Court trials are jury trials, presided over by a judge who may be a High Court judge, a circuit judge or a recorder. The judge directs the jury on the law and on the weight to be attached to the evidence of each witness. The jury decides whether the defendant is guilty or not guilty. If the defendant is convicted, the judge passes sentence, usually after an adjournment for pre-sentence reports.

*Correct Form of Address*

This depends on the status of the judge. Ask the usher or the lawyers. All judges sitting in the Crown Court (circuit judges, recorders and assistant recorders) are addressed as "Your Honour" except High Court (or red) judges and any judge sitting at the Old Bailey in London or in the Court of the Recorder of Liverpool or Manchester. These judges are all addressed as "Your Lordship/Ladyship" or "My Lord/Lady". A High Court judge is often referred to as a "red judge" because their formal court attire is coloured red (and black). On the court list, a High Court judge's surname is always followed by the abbreviation "J", as opposed to the abbreviation "HHJ" used for circuit judges.

## The High Court

Appeals from the Magistrates' Court or the Crown Court may sometimes be heard in the Queen's Bench Division of the High Court.

*Who Sits*

One High Court judge and one Lord Justice of Appeal.

*Correct Form of Address*

"Your Lordship/Ladyship" or "My Lord/Lady".

## The Court of Appeal

The Criminal Division hears appeals from the Crown Court on points of law and also appeals against sentence by the prosecution or the defence.

*Who Sits*

Usually three, but sometimes two, judges. At least one of these judges must be a Lord Justice of Appeal. The other judges may be either two further Lords Justices of Appeal, two High Court judges or one High Court judge and one circuit judge. The Lord Chief Justice is a Lord Justice of Appeal. He is also the head of the Criminal Division of the Supreme Court and is the most senior criminal judge in England and Wales.

*Correct Form of Address*

"Your Lordship/Ladyship" or "My Lord/Lady".

## The House of Lords

Like the Court of Appeal, the House of Lords is exclusively appellate. It hears appeals from the Court of Appeal (Criminal Division) and also (exceptionally) from the Queen's Bench Division of the High Court.

*Who Sits*

From three to seven, but usually five, Lords of Appeal.

*Correct Form of Address*

"Your Lordship/Ladyship" or "My Lord/Lady".

## PARTIES TO PROCEEDINGS IN THE CRIMINAL COURTS

### The Prosecution

The State/Crown, through the Crown Prosecution Service, prosecute people for allegedly committing crimes. Examples of such crimes are fraud, theft, burglary, robbery, rape, assaults against the person, murder, manslaughter, dangerous driving, drug smuggling, etc. Exceptionally, an individual victim may bring a private prosecution.

At the trial, the prosecution's case against the defendant is heard first.

### The Defence

The defendant in a criminal trial is the person whom the prosecution alleges has committed a criminal offence. Criminal offences are set out in statutes, i.e. Acts of Parliament, or exist as common law offences, that is they are offences that have been created by judges in decided cases. The defendant may be found "guilty" or "not guilty". This is a decision made by the jury in the Crown Court and by the magistrates in the Magistrates' Court. Sentences may be custodial or non-custodial, i.e. the defendant can be imprisoned or given a sentence falling short of imprisonment such as a fine or a community sentence.

### THE BURDEN AND STANDARD OF PROOF

Generally the burden or onus of proof rests on the prosecution. They have to show that there is sufficient evidence to convict the defendant. The prosecution is required to prove every fact in issue to a high standard, that is beyond reasonable doubt, in order to secure a conviction.

This burden extends not only to proving every element of the offence but also to disproving the defendant's defence. The aim is to get to the truth of what happened. This means that, in situations where the defendant wishes to rely on a defence such as self-defence, provocation or duress, it is for the prosecution to disprove these defences beyond reasonable doubt.

There are a few occasions where the burden of proof falls on the defence. For example, where the defendant wishes to plead insanity or diminished responsibility, the defence must prove it. However, the defence is only required to prove such a defence on the balance of probability (rather than beyond reasonable doubt).

When the prosecution must prove their case beyond reasonable doubt, the jury or magistrates should convict only if they are sure that the defendant is guilty. By contrast, where the defence is required to prove its defence on the balance of probability, the jury or magistrates should accept this defence only if they are satisfied that the defence is more likely to be true than not.

## HOW CRIMINAL CASES START

Investigation and prosecution of criminal cases is funded by the State. Criminal cases start with an investigation by the police, HM Revenue and Customs, the Serious Fraud Office (SFO) or the Department of Trade and Industry (DTI). If, after investigation, it is believed that an individual has committed an offence, then one of two courses will be followed.

In cases where it is not deemed necessary to arrest the offender, a summons is served advising them that it is believed that they have committed a criminal offence. Alternatively, the individual will be arrested and then, usually after a police interview, will be formally charged. In each case they will then be committed to court to be tried.

Offences are classified into three types in criminal proceedings: summary, "either way" and indictable. Trials of summary only offences, that is less serious offences, always take place in the Magistrates' Court. Trials of indictable only offences, the most serious offences such as murder, take place in the Crown Court.

Trials of "either way" offences such as theft may, however, take place in either the Crown Court or the Magistrates' Court. The magistrates decide at a Mode of Trial hearing whether the case is suitable to be tried in the Magistrates' Court or in the Crown Court. If the former, the magistrates will continue with the hearing to try the offence.

When the Magistrates' Court decides that an "either way" offence is to be tried at the Crown Court, and in the case of all indictable only offences, there will be a **committal** hearing in the Magistrates' Court.

This is a hearing to send the defendant to the Crown Court for trial, if the prosecution have sufficient evidence for there to be a "case to answer", that is that there is sufficient prosecution evidence to warrant the case being listed for trial in the Crown Court.

Thus the initial proceedings for all cases take place in the Magistrates' Court.

A full trial of indictable only offences and "either way" offences committed to the Crown Court will take place at Crown Court unless the defendant pleads guilty. If the defendant pleads guilty, the Crown Court will move on to consider sentencing. If the defendant pleads not guilty but is found guilty, sentencing will usually take place on a different day.

The magistrates decide if a defendant is entitled to be released on bail pending trial, or whether the defendant will be held in custody to await trial. They also decide if the defendant is entitled to have legal aid to defend the case. This decision will be based partly on the means of the defendant and partly on whether it is in the "interests of justice" that the defendant should receive legal aid.

Appeals may be made to the higher courts from the Magistrates' Court or the Crown Court. The following diagram shows the full procedure in criminal cases, including the appeals structure.

# Criminal Litigation: An Overview of the Procedure and Appeal System

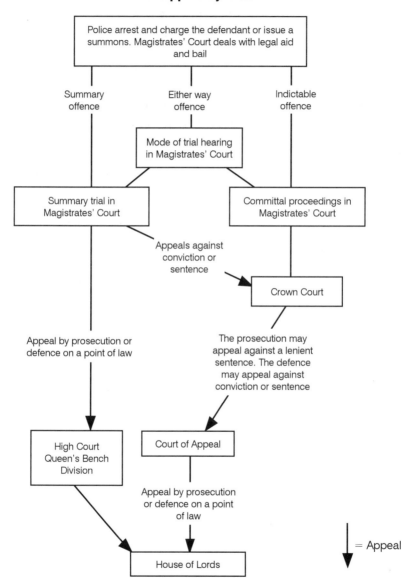

## EVIDENCE IN CRIMINAL TRIALS

The key to the adversarial system is the testing of evidence. This allows the court to decide how much weight or credit to attach to each piece of evidence.

There are many detailed rules of evidence. An expert does not need to know all these and should feel free to ask the lawyers which rules are relevant. There are, however, some rules which it is useful to understand.

Evidence can be divided into three categories: documentary evidence, real evidence and witness evidence.

Documentary evidence includes such things as photographs, photofits, and video and tape recordings. Documents have to be proved to be authentic which means that a witness may have to be called to give oral evidence to explain how a document came into existence.

Examples of real evidence are a knife, a gun and a piece of paper with the defendant's signature on.

### Discovery/Disclosure of Evidence

Disclosure of evidence means letting the other party know what evidence you have.

A party to criminal proceedings in the Crown Court who is going to call expert evidence at trial is required to give advance disclosure of the content of this evidence to all other parties. This disclosure must be given after committal to the Crown Court for trial. If such advance disclosure is not given, then the oral or written evidence of the expert cannot be given at Crown Court without the leave (permission) of the judge. A judge will only grant leave if he or she thinks it is fair to do so.

If the trial is in the Magistrates' Court, there is not a formal obligation to give advance disclosure of expert evidence to any other party. However, it will often be disclosed to avoid an opponent having to ask for an adjournment during the trial to get their own expert opinion.

### Witness Summons

A witness summons is a written order from the court demanding the attendance of a witness.

Witnesses will be asked to confirm in writing that they will attend court to give oral evidence at a trial. If no reply is received or if the witness refuses to attend, then the solicitor will write to the court explaining that they have not been able to secure voluntary attendance of a witness. To make sure the witness comes to court, the court will order them to by issuing a witness summons.

The solicitor for either party to a case can apply to the court for a witness summons to be issued to each witness, whether an expert witness or a witness as to fact, who is required to give oral evidence at court and will not otherwise attend. A witness summons will be served personally on the witness. It will tell the witness where and when they must go. If a witness fails to attend after receiving a witness summons they may be arrested, brought to court and fined and/or imprisoned as a punishment for their failure to comply with the summons.

As far as witness evidence is concerned, there are three types of witnesses: witnesses of fact, professional witnesses and expert witnesses.

### WITNESSES OF FACT

A witness of fact is someone who is called to give evidence about what happened in a case. They are there to recall what they saw, heard or did during an incident but not to give opinions. They are required to discuss the facts they remember or recorded in notes. Examples of such witnesses are a witness to a fight; a nurse in a hospital who saw a patient in casualty and recorded details of their injuries; a police officer who made notes in his/her notebook; a witness who gives identification evidence.

A witness as to fact *must* give oral evidence at the trial unless the opposing party agrees that the witness's statement may be read instead. They may only testify to those things that they heard or saw themselves and not to anything that they were told happened by a third party. Such "second hand" evidence is classified as hearsay and is not admissible.

While in the witness box, a witness may refresh their memory from any contemporaneous records they have kept. Contemporaneous records are records completed while the facts were still fresh in the witness's mind. Such a contemporaneous note may be read out by the witness as part of the oral evidence. The note may be questioned and inspected by the "opposing" party to the trial.

Examples of such notes are a police officer's notebook, a scientist's record of experiments into drugs, chemicals or handwriting, and medical records. It is important to keep accurate full notes containing the following type of information:

— Dates, start and finish time, location.

— Who was present, e.g. researcher, patient, client.

— Examination/experiment and finding.

— Details of facts observed and opinions (the latter if you will be an expert witness as well as a witness as to fact).

— Details of advice given/conversations.

A witness as to fact is not entitled to sit in court and listen to other witnesses' evidence before they give their evidence.

**Witness of Fact Statement in Criminal Trials**

Witnesses of fact do not write reports but make statements.

A statement will usually be written some time after the event to which it refers and usually at the prompting of a police officer or a solicitor. Its purpose is to set out in writing the witness's recollection of the events in question in as much detail as possible using the witness's memory and/or notes taken at the time. The statement itself is not the witness's evidence. This evidence is given orally from the witness box. A witness of fact may use their notes as a memory refreshing document. The witness must state that the notes contain their record of events at the time the notes were made and that this earlier recollection is likely to be significantly better than the recollection which can be given at the time of giving evidence. Although the new rules in the Criminal Justice Act 2003 (which came into force in 2005) do not require the notes to be "contemporaneous" the meaning of "significantly" is highly likely to be affected by how long after the incident the notes were made. Following the Criminal Justice Act 2003, a witness of fact in criminal proceedings may refer to their statement in the witness box if they are able to satisfy the "significantly" test.

A witness statement which does not satisfy the "significantly" test is used both to refresh the witness's memory outside the witness box and to allow both parties to see what the witness's evidence is prior to trial. There must be no ambush evidence.

In the following situations, the witness statement can be used as evidence *without* the need to call the witness to give oral evidence.

1. As a section 9 statement under the Criminal Justice Act 1967. This is where a signed witness statement, which has been served on

the other party in advance of the trial, can be admitted as evidence because the other party has read it and has decided they do not wish to cross-examine the witness and they do not object to the witness statement being read in court. In this case there is no need for the witness to give oral evidence in the witness box. This procedure is commonly used where the witness merely gives formal evidence, for example a relative of the deceased identifying the body in a murder case. But if the other party does object to the section 9 statement being read out, the witness must give oral evidence. The purpose of a section 9 statement is to avoid the time and expense of a witness going to court when this is unnecessary.

The declaration at the top of a section 9 statement reads "This statement, consisting of x pages, is true to the best of my knowledge and belief and I make it knowing that, if it is tendered in evidence, I shall be liable to prosecution if I have wilfully stated in it anything which I know to be false or do not believe to be true."

2. The statement was made by someone who is now dead, or unfit to attend as a witness, or is outside the United Kingdom and it is not reasonably practicable to secure their attendance, or the statement was made to the police and the person refuses to give evidence through fear.

3. The witness has recorded observations in a business document or record of accounts or they are stored in a computer.

**Do Witnesses of Fact Get Paid?**

Witnesses of fact do not get paid for giving evidence but they may claim their travelling expenses. A number of people give factual evidence as part of their job, for example police officers and traffic wardens.

## EXPERT WITNESSES

An expert witness will give evidence of both **facts** and **opinion**.

### Evidence of Facts

Facts fall into two different categories.

1. There are those facts which the expert has observed himself, such as handwriting, a concrete base, a broken leg, skid marks on a road.

2. There are those facts that an expert has been told, such as the level of pain, mental injury caused, the distance from which a rifle was fired, or facts observed from documents or real evidence. Included in this category of facts are facts that have been reported to the expert by a member of his/her research team.

The facts which will be given most weight by the court will be those observed by experts themselves. However, the court is allowed to take into account other facts which experts have relied on to come to their expert opinion. Of course, most of the facts relied on will have to be tested by the oral cross-examination of witnesses as to fact. The expert should clearly identify the source of the facts, e.g. "I have been told by Mr. X that ..." or "At about 11.00 a.m. on 10th July 1997 at Greenway Police Station I examined the accused and I saw that he had bruising around the left eye."

### Evidence of Opinion

Expert opinion evidence is admissible on matters not within the common knowledge of the court. The reason for an expert witness being asked to give evidence is because the court does not know or understand matters within certain fields. They need the help of an expert to understand the case. Experts are entitled to give opinion evidence because of their qualifications and experience in their particular field of expertise. For example, a scientist who examines a suspicious substance may say that in his expert opinion it has all the characteristics of cannabis. Expertise may exist in a wide range of fields including medicine, science, technology, environmental issues, pension funds, loss of earnings, etc.

## The Role of the Expert Witness

In criminal trials expert witnesses will often be giving their opinion on whether or not the defendant was involved in the offence or any element of it. It is essential for the expert witness to know what offence the defendant is charged with and what the likely defence is.

For example, in a robbery, where the defendant is putting forward a defence that he or she was not at the scene of the crime, a forensic scientist may be giving evidence of their own analysis of the DNA found in hairs collected at the scene of the crime, and may say that, in their opinion, this analysis shows that it is statistically probable that the defendant was at the scene of the crime.

A psychiatrist or a psychologist may give evidence as to what type of sentence is most appropriate for the defendant following the defendant's conviction.

In a murder case, a doctor may give medical evidence on whether or not the defendant had a state of mind which a jury could find amounted to a defence of diminished responsibility or insanity.

**Remember, an expert witness gives evidence of both fact and opinion.** For instance, in the DNA example above, the evidence about the carrying out of the DNA analysis and its results is evidence of *fact*, whereas the evidence about the statistical probability of the defendant being present at the scene is *opinion* evidence. Opinion evidence must be based on a foundation of factual evidence.

## Expert Reports

Experts will generally write a report, unlike witnesses as to fact and professional witnesses who make statements. A report is a written document which sets out what the facts are and what the expert's opinion is. Chapter 3 deals with the writing of experts' reports and there is an example of an expert's report in the appendices.

It is possible for the court to read an expert's written report even though the expert does not attend the trial, if the other party agrees it is not necessary for the expert to give oral evidence or the court gives leave for the report to be admissible without the expert's attendance. However, a court usually gives more weight to the expert's evidence when the expert attends the trial and gives evidence orally and that evidence is subjected to rigorous testing under cross-examination.

An expert is entitled to take their report into the witness box and refer to it while giving evidence. They should have a clean copy of the report and should not take in an annotated copy.

## Privilege for Expert's Report Prepared for the Defendant

Privilege means that a report is protected from public general knowledge. The existence and content of the report can only be known to the expert, the instructing solicitor and the solicitor's client.

Communications between a defendant or their solicitor and an expert are privileged, so long as they were made in contemplation of pending litigation. If a document (for example a letter, a record of a telephone call, or a draft or final version of an expert's report) is privileged, then the defence cannot be compelled to reveal it to the prosecution. An expert's report that is unfavourable to the accused and is not going to be used at trial need never be disclosed, that is revealed, to the other party(ies).

## Discovery/Disclosure of Expert's Report Prepared for the Defendant

There is a general rule that trials cannot be conducted by ambush, so once a party decides it is going to rely on a piece of evidence at trial, it must be revealed to the other side. At this stage, known as disclosure, the privilege over the report is lost. The report is disclosed or revealed to the other side.

If an expert report is going to be relied on by the defence at the Crown Court, it must be disclosed to the prosecution. Once the defence has disclosed an expert's report to the prosecution (whether the case is to be heard in the Crown Court or in the Magistrates' Court), the defence is deemed to have waived the privilege in the report. In the Magistrates' Court it is usual for the defence to disclose all the experts' reports on which they propose to rely well in advance of the trial. This avoids the trial court having to grant the prosecution an adjournment during the trial in order to give the prosecution the opportunity to deal with this expert evidence (by instructing and calling an expert of its own).

***Under Part 24 of the Criminal Procedure Rules, both prosecution and defence must provide each other with expert evidence to be relied on at trial and, on request, provide supporting evidence. There should be no surprise evidence.***

- Note that any records or accounts that were prepared for reasons other than litigation do not enjoy privilege and are liable to be disclosed to the other side.

- The duty on the prosecution to disclose unused/unfavourable evidence is more onerous than on the defence.

## PROFESSIONAL WITNESSES

Most professional witnesses give evidence as a result of seeing something happen in the course of their everyday job. Giving evidence about it is also part of their job. The best examples are police officers and police surgeons.

Professional witnesses can give some opinion evidence. However, they often give a lot of factual evidence. Their evidence is in the form of a statement, not a report. If the evidence they give is not disputed by the other party, it may be given as a section 9 statement. This means the evidence will be read in court without the need for them to give oral evidence.

Professional witnesses are classified separately for purposes of payment of fees only.

## PROCEDURE OF A CRIMINAL TRIAL

1. Prosecution opening speech.

2. Prosecution call their evidence first.

    For each witness: Examination in chief (by prosecution)

    Cross-examination (by defence)

    Re-examination (by prosecution).

3. At the end of the prosecution case, the defence may make a submission of "no case to answer" if the prosecution evidence cannot be relied on and they cannot prove key elements of the offence charged. If the court agrees there is no case to answer, the defendant will be set free. If there is a case to answer then:

4. Defence opening speech.

5. Defence call their evidence.

    For each witness: Examination in chief (by defence)

    Cross-examination (by prosecution)

    Re-examination (by defence).

6. Defence closing speech.

Prosecution may have a closing speech (in Crown Court but rarely in Magistrates' Court).

In a criminal trial, the witnesses of fact may not sit in court and listen to other witnesses' evidence before they give their own evidence. However, expert witnesses may sit in court and listen to all the evidence.

# *The Civil Courts*

## COURT STRUCTURE

There are two civil courts in which cases are commenced and trials are held, the County Court and the High Court. However, it should be noted that the vast majority of civil litigation cases (96%) are settled before they come to trial.

Proceedings for money claims (except personal injury) can only be started in the High Court where the amount in dispute is more than £15,000. However, the High Court may transfer the more straightforward cases about slightly larger amounts to the County Court. County Courts may also transfer cases to other County Courts, usually for the convenience of one or both parties.

Proceedings in respect of personal injury litigation must be commenced in the County Court, unless the value of the action is £50,000 or more in which case proceedings may be started in the High Court. However, there is no limit to the damages that can be awarded in the County Court. In practice, therefore, most personal injury actions are started in the County Court even if they are worth more than £50,000.

### The County Court

The sort of cases heard in the County Court are debt and contract claims, building disputes, claims for faulty goods and services, personal injury litigation, landlord and tenant litigation and professional negligence claims.

*Who Sits*

Trials in which the sum in issue is less than £5,000 are heard by a district judge. Actions where the sum in issue is more than £5,000 but less than £15,000 are heard by a district judge, a circuit judge, recorder or assistant recorder. Actions where the sum in issue is more than £15,000 are heard by a circuit judge, recorder or assistant recorder.

Trials and many shorter hearings in the County Courts are open to the public.

*Correct Form of Address*

A district judge, recorder and assistant recorder are addressed as "Sir" or "Madam". A circuit judge is addressed as "Your Honour".

## Arbitration

Arbitration is an adjudication process operating outside the court system in which a third party will reach a decision which is binding on the parties. Procedure at arbitration hearings may be less formal than in the courts and will be decided by the arbitrator to suit the needs of the case. Hearings are usually in private and the decision of the arbitrator is likely to be confidential. The arbitrator, who is chosen by the parties, may be a lawyer or other professional who is an expert in a particular field and will understand the issues at stake. For example, a construction engineer may be the arbitrator in a building dispute. Expert witnesses and other witnesses may give evidence at the hearing.

## Alternative Dispute Resolution (ADR)

This is a term which describes a number of different processes which are an alternative to litigation through the civil court system. The purpose of ADR is to enable parties to settle their disputes outside the courtroom, often by using a third party to assist. Mediation is the most frequently used approach, in which an independent neutral person works with the parties to help them reach a solution. Mediators may be lawyers, other professionals or people with the requisite skills who have undertaken the necessary training. The mediator does not make a decision; it is up to the parties to try to reach a settlement. The outcome is not binding unless the parties decide it shall be. Mediations are held in private.

The advantage of mediation and other forms of ADR is that it is often quicker, cheaper and less formal than court proceedings. It is particularly suitable for parties who wish to retain a (working) relationship after the dispute is over and/or want their disputes settled confidentially.

Sometimes a contract between two parties will provide for arbitration or ADR in the event of a dispute. Alternatively, the parties can simply agree to use ADR instead of, or during, litigation through the court system. The courts are increasingly pro-active in encouraging the parties to use ADR and may impose costs sanctions on a party who unreasonably refuses to participate in ADR.

The civil courts also have the power to order proceedings to be "stayed" while the parties try to reach a settlement, including by ADR.

## The High Court

The High Court has three divisions:

1. Queen's Bench Division (which includes the Commercial Court and the Admiralty Court) – breach of contract, larger personal injury, negligence, insurance and judicial review are the main claims.

2. Chancery Division (which includes the Companies Court and the Patents Court) – banking and financial services disputes, trusts, probate, land disputes, partnership action.

3. Family Division – wardship, adoption, guardianship.

*Who Sits*

Usually one High Court judge, but it can be a circuit judge or senior QC.

In cases of libel, slander, malicious prosecution and unlawful imprisonment, a *jury* will usually sit with the judge. The jury will make the decisions of fact; the judge will direct the proceedings.

*Correct Form of Address*

"Your Lordship/Ladyship" or "My Lord/Lady".

## The Court of Appeal (Civil Division)

Only important civil cases go to the Court of Appeal. Appeals are heard from the High Court, the County Court and certain tribunals with permission, either from the judge who tried the case or from the Court of Appeal. The jurisdiction is entirely appellate, which means that no new evidence can be presented. Documents will be read and legal argument presented. The decision may be by a majority.

*Who Sits*

Usually three Lords Justice of Appeal. These may include the Lord Chief Justice, the Master of the Rolls or the Vice Chancellor.

*Correct Form of Address*

"Your Lordship/Ladyship" or "My Lord/Lady".

## The House of Lords

Sits in the committee rooms in the Houses of Parliament at Westminster.

The House of Lords only hears cases where there is a principle of law that is of great public importance. The House of Lords listens only to legal argument.

*Who Sits*

Between three and seven, but usually five, Lords of Appeal will sit. Sometimes the Lord Chancellor will preside.

*Correct Form of Address*

"Your Lordship/Ladyship" or "My Lord/Lady".

## Magistrates' Court

Generally, Magistrates' Courts deal with criminal cases but they also deal with family matters and licensing.

*Correct Form of Address*
"Sir/Madam".

## Tribunals

There are many separate tribunals which hear specialist pages within the civil justice system. For example, there are employment tribunals which hear disputes about employment law rights and issues, social security tribunals and immigration tribunals. Proceedings in tribunals are less formal than in court. There is usually a panel of three people (one of whom is usually a lawyer) who decide the cases.

## THE TRACKING SYSTEM IN THE CIVIL COURTS

Since April 1999, when the Civil Procedure Rules were implemented, all claims which are defended are allocated to one of three case management "tracks" in which different procedures and degrees of "judicial management" are followed to suit the needs and value of the claim. The Small Claims and Fast Tracks are part of the County Court; the Multi Track may be managed by district judges in the County Court but the trial will be heard by a circuit or High Court judge.

The Small Claims Track is the normal track for claims up to £5,000. It is also for personal injury claims of a value up to £5,000 where the personal injury element is not more than £1,000, and for housing disrepair claims of £1,000 or less. Hearings are informal so that they can be conducted without a lawyer, and the loser is not ordered to pay all the winner's costs – usually only the court fee and witnesses' expenses. The judge will only rarely ask for expert evidence and then usually only as a written report.

The Fast Track is the normal track for other claims up to £15,000 where the matter is not complex and the trial can be heard in one day. The government is working towards a system of fixed costs, recoverable by the winning party from the loser and has introduced fixed costs schemes for specific types of claims, for example, road traffic accidents and employers' liability claims. Generally, for other types of fast track cases, some of the costs are fixed, (for example, the fees of the advocate appearing at the trial are on a scale of £350–£750).

The Multi Track is the normal track for claims over £15,000 or for lower value claims which are too complicated to be tried in one day and which merit more "hands on" management by a judge.

The court (usually a district judge or High Court Master) decides to which track a case should be allocated, if and when it is defended. The parties fill in a detailed questionnaire which includes such information as the number of witnesses of fact, whether expert witnesses may be needed and the steps to prepare the case for trial.

The intention in the civil justice reforms is that all Small Claims and Fast Track cases will be concluded within 30 weeks of their allocation to a track, much more quickly than under the previous system. Multi Track cases have their own individual timetables but should reach trial in 1–2 years – also a considerable improvement on what went before.

## PARTIES TO THE PROCEEDINGS IN THE CIVIL COURTS

Litigation is between the claimant and the defendant. Each party sets out their case in writing (statements of case), giving details of what happened, allegations against the other party, any points of law in dispute, an outline of their evidence and (for the claimant) what the party wants as a remedy.

### The Claimant

A claimant is someone who starts a court action. Usually, they believe that they have suffered a wrongful loss. For example, they believe that the other party to a contract has broken it, or they have been physically injured in a road traffic accident or in an accident at work, or have been given poor professional advice. The claimant wants to claim money from the person or organisation who caused the loss and brings a court action (sues) to obtain financial compensation in the form of *damages* from a defendant, if and when the defendant refuses to settle the dispute without court proceedings.

Most claimants instruct lawyers to help them bring their case. There are three things that the claimant has to show to the court:

1. That the defendant, the person being sued, is responsible for the claimant's loss or damage. This is known as liability.

2. That the defendant's actions caused the claimant's losses. This is known as causation.

3. If liability and causation can be established, the *amount* of money that is due (this is called *quantum*, a Latin word meaning amount). The amount of money awarded is to compensate the claimant (as far as money can) for their loss.

Expert witnesses may be asked to give their opinion on liability, causation or quantum, or a combination of these.

For example, a surveyor may be asked to give an opinion as to the cause of a roof collapsing: whether it was due to adverse weather conditions or inadequate support beams in the roof (liability). He or she may also be asked to give his/her opinion on the amount of damages (quantum) the claimant should recover to compensate the claimant for the collapsed roof. The surveyor may be asked to estimate how much it will cost the claimant to rebuild the roof.

At the trial, the claimant's case will usually be heard first.

## The Defendant

The defendant is a person or organisation from whom money or another remedy is claimed, for example a motorist who has run over a pedestrian and injured him or an employer at whose premises an employee was injured. Money compensation is called damages. If the claimant wins the case, then an order to pay damages will often be made. The losing defendant is not "guilty", but merely said to be liable to the claimant and judgment is entered against them. When the defendant is insured, the defence will usually be run by the insurance company.

## THE BURDEN AND STANDARD OF PROOF

The burden of proving a fact lies with the party bringing the action, the claimant. So, if a claimant is alleging professional negligence, then the claimant must prove all the elements of the tort of negligence. The issues that arise are:

(i) That a duty of care existed between the claimant and the defendant.

(ii) That the defendant breached this duty of care.

(iii) That the breach caused the claimant's loss/damage.

(iv) The amount of this loss/damage.

In civil cases, the claimant is required to prove their case "on the balance of probabilities". This is an easier burden than the "beyond reasonable doubt" required in criminal cases. It means that the judge must be persuaded that the claimant's version of events is more likely to be true than the defendant's.

If a defendant brings a counterclaim against the claimant, e.g. in a road traffic claim that the claimant damaged the defendant's vehicle, the defendant has to prove the facts and issues in their part of the case. Here the standard of proof is also on the balance of probabilities.

## Civil Litigation: Overview of the Procedure

Information collected – possibly including
preliminary advice from an expert

Pre-action contact between the parties
- letter of claim and response
  - attempts to settle

Issue of proceedings
- claim form + particulars of claim

Defence (and counterclaim)

Allocation by the court to a case management
track and directions/timetable up to trial

Exchange of evidence
- disclosure of documents
  - witness statements
- experts' reports – where court requires these

Court fixes definite trial date and reviews readiness
for trial

Trial

(Appeal to Court of Appeal/House of Lords)

## HOW CIVIL CASES START

### The Expert's Role

The expert's role in civil claims has changed fundamentally because of Lord Woolf's reforms. He concluded that, in many cases, expert evidence was not necessary and/or was too expensive and contributed to delay, and that some experts were too "partisan" and tended to act as advocates for "their" client's case, instead of as a "neutral fact finder or opinion giver" to help the court.

Before starting a civil case, the claimant with their legal advisers (if any) will have to decide whether he/she has a worthwhile case, whether the defendant will be able to pay if the claimant succeeds and whether the likely value of the claim justifies the likely cost of investigating and proving it.

An expert may have an important role to play at this stage. Experts may be asked to provide advice or a "preliminary report". This is to help the claimant decide if he/she has a case worth bringing against the defendant; and, perhaps, to help the solicitor to decide whether to take on the case, especially if he or she is thinking about running it on a "no win no fee" basis. At this stage, the expert's role is as an adviser, not as an expert witness.

The claimant and their solicitors may have obtained statements from witnesses of fact as to who saw and heard the incident in question.

It is important that the expert adviser exercises clear, independent judgment when writing a preliminary report. The claimant and solicitor need to know all the weaknesses of the case as well as the strengths. If the expert writes an unfavourable report, then the solicitor may advise the client not to pursue the case.

If the client still wishes to go ahead, usually there will be no need for the expert's advisory report, whether it is unfavourable or not, to be revealed to the other side. This is because only an expert's report that has been jointly commissioned with the other party, or has been obtained with the permission of the court for use in evidence in proceedings, will have to be disclosed to the other side. Unfavourable advisory initial reports which are not used remain privileged, that is they remain confidential to the client, the expert and the client's solicitor. However, the client will not be able to recover the costs of the report from the other party, even if he or she is successful in the litigation at the end of the day.

Many different types of experts may be used in civil claims, e.g. engineers, psychologists, psychiatrists, doctors, scientists, accountants, surveyors, etc.

### The Civil Justice Reforms – Emphasis on "Litigation as a Last Resort" and the Pre-action Protocols

One of the most important changes introduced by the Civil Procedure Rules in 1999 was the requirement for the parties to exchange information about their dispute before issuing proceedings. These procedures are set out in a series of Pre-Action Protocols applicable to different types of disputes (for example, Personal Injury claims, Construction and Engineering Disputes and Professional Negligence claims) and there is also a general protocol which applies to cases where there is no specific protocol.

All the Protocols have similar procedures. Potential claimants are now expected to send to the potential defendant as soon as possible a detailed letter of claim which sets out their version of the events and gives the defendant sufficient information to carry out their own investigation, and to take a view on whether to admit liability and on how much the claim might be worth. The claimant should allow the defendant a reasonable time to reply before starting proceedings – in most cases, the timetable is set out in the relevant protocol.

If the defendant accepts liability, the parties should try to settle the case and this may mean obtaining a report from an expert to help resolve the amount of damages.

If the defendant does not accept liability, the parties should, nonetheless, try to work together to exchange information, including essential documents, and by co-operating on the expert evidence which may be needed. The intention is that litigation should be seen as "a last resort" which should only be started when the parties have all the relevant information to hand to enable them to decide whether to commence proceedings or not and all the possibilities of resolving the dispute without recourse to litigation have been explored.

The personal injury pre-action protocol (which is designed for Fast Track type claims in particular) specifically requires the parties to try to agree to instruct one shared medical (or any other) expert, rather than one expert each, to save time and cost. The expert instructed is not a joint expert but is instructed by the claimant; the report is disclosed to the defendant who is invited to agree to it. If the parties cannot agree and the case proceeds to litigation, the court may penalise the party who was unreasonable (usually in costs), even if he/she wins the case.

An expert who is instructed to act on this basis at an early stage in a claim should be aware that he/she may receive written questions on their report from one or both parties.

## PRE-ACTION DISCLOSURE AND INSPECTION

Before the case is formally started in court, each side may need to know and see what documents, photographs, etc. the other side has. The parties should try to agree and should exchange documents on an amicable basis. The pre-action protocols require this.

However, if the parties cannot agree, one or both may need to apply to the court for pre-action disclosure (that is, to know of the existence of documents which the other party has in their custody, possession or control), which the applicant party needs to decide if they assist the dispute in being resolved without proceedings, dispose fairly of anticipated proceedings or to save costs.

A party may also need pre-action inspection (the right to see) the property of the other party or a third party. An expert will often have to make arrangements to see a patient, or visit the scene of an accident to do sketches and take photographs.

The court rules allow parties to make similar applications to see the documents or inspect the property of a third party who is not involved in the case, but only if it is necessary to dispose of the claim fairly or to save costs. It is only possible to obtain documents where the disclosure is likely to support the case of the applicant or to adversely affect the case of another party to the proceedings. The rule cannot be used as a "fishing expedition".

## ISSUE OF PROCEEDINGS

The issue of proceedings is the formal process by which litigation is started in the court system. Before issuing proceedings, the claimant's solicitor will send a "letter before action" or letter of claim. This will explain the basis of the claim, including the amount of damages (in outline) and will serve as notice that proceedings may be issued if the defendant disputes the claim and a settlement cannot be reached.

The issue of proceedings involves the solicitor sending or taking a **claim form** and (within 14 days) **particulars of claim** (which set out the details of the case against the defendant) and a fee to the court. The court will enter an action number on the claim form after sealing it with the court seal. Since April 1999 there is only one claim form for all types of claim, whether they are to be pursued in the County or High Court.

In personal injury and some other types of cases, the solicitor may also be required to file at court an initial expert's report – in particular a medical report and the calculation of special damages. The claim form, particulars of claim (and, if appropriate, medical report and the calculation of special damages) will then be served on the defendant by the court unless the claimant obtains the court's permission to serve them.

## STATEMENTS OF CASE

Statements of case are documents (often legally drafted) which set out what happened and what the parties want – they are the arguments put forward by the parties. The object of statements of case is to define the issues which the parties want the court to decide. They give each party notice of the issues to be contested and the facts that will be raised. The claim form and the particulars of claim are the first formal court documents. It enables the defendant to see the case against it.

After service of the claim form and particulars of claim, the defendant decides whether to admit the claim or to put in a **defence** and, if appropriate, a **counterclaim**. (A counterclaim is when the defendant alleges that the claimant's conduct has caused the defendant loss and damage.) This enables the claimant to see the case against it. The claimant may file a **reply** to the defence and, if appropriate, a defence to counterclaim.

The Civil Procedure Rules encourage both parties to be concise but specific in their statements of case.

The claimant's claim form must contain:

- A concise statement of the nature of the claim and the remedy sought.

- A statement of the likely value of the claim (partly to assist the court in allocating the case to a track if it is defended).

- A statement of truth which is a statement that the claimant believes that the facts stated are true.

The full particulars of claim should also include:

- The claimant's version of the relevant events.

- The specific allegations against the defendant.

- Reference to any applicable law.

It may include, or annex, relevant evidence, e.g. documents on which the claim is based and/or witness statements.

A defendant must respond to the particulars of claim within 14 days of receipt. He can choose to:

- Admit all or part of the claim.

- Defend it (and possibly counterclaim).

- Acknowledge service and then follow this up within 14 days with either an admission or a defence unless the claimant will agree an extension of time, which can only be up to 28 days without the court's express permission.

The rules specifically require defendants to answer all the claimant's allegations, with reasons. "Holding" or "bare denial" defences will now be rejected by the courts. Defences must also include a statement of truth.

In fact the court has wide powers to strike out any statement of case, by either claimant or defendant, which does not comply with the rules or does not disclose a real claim or defence.

In personal injury cases, if the defendant disputes the claimant's medical report or schedule of losses, he should say so, again giving details and reasons.

In some "technical" cases, particularly professional negligence claims, experts may have an important role in advising on drafting the statements of case.

### Requests for Further Information

Either party may request more details about the other party's case. Experts may be asked to help the solicitors in deciding what to ask.

## CASE MANAGEMENT BY THE COURT

The civil justice reforms place on the courts a new duty to manage and control all cases in accordance with the "overriding objective", a set of guiding principles set out in CPR Part 1, and with the specific case management powers, summarised in CPR Parts 3 and 26, and with regard to the rules for the separate tracks set out in CPR Parts 27-29.

These important changes are designed to ensure cases no longer drift or take several years to reach a conclusion and to prevent the work and costs becoming disproportionate to the amount in dispute.

The court's specific case management powers include:

- Ordering a stay of proceedings for one month, or any other period that it considers appropriate, to allow parties to try to settle by negotiation or mediation.

- Working with the parties to try to narrow the areas in dispute.

- Taking some decisions "on paper" without a hearing, or by holding telephone hearings.

- Imposing penalties on parties who do not comply with the rules or with court orders and directions – this might be payment of both sides' costs of a particular step regardless of the outcome of the case, or precluding the party in default from relying on evidence served late.

- Controlling the costs by setting budgets or limiting the amount which can be recovered from the other side, including experts' fees.

A judge will look at each case which is defended, once the allocation questionnaires are returned, and will usually:

- Allocate the case to a track.

- Set a trial date or period within which the trial will take place; for Small and Fast Track claims this will be about 30 weeks ahead and, for Multi Track, 1–2 years.

- Give directions for the conduct of the case until trial, including a timetable for serving the evidence.

In more complex cases, or those running into difficulties, the judge will arrange a **case management conference**, to be attended by the lawyers – and often the parties too, to plan how the dispute will get to trial or be resolved without spending more resources on the case than it merits. This might involve a short hearing to dispose of the case without a full trial (summary judgment) or to deal with specific issues, e.g. liability, but not quantum.

These court powers and rules have had a significant impact on expert witnesses and their evidence: especially the much tighter timetables. Experts have to be able to prepare reports in smaller cases in a matter of weeks and to advise on, and prepare witness statements for, hearings for interim payments and summary judgments to a very tight timetable.

## EXCHANGE OF EVIDENCE

The purpose of exchange of evidence is to avoid surprise evidence at trial. There can be no trial by ambush any longer. Each party is entitled to see the evidence of the other party weeks or months before trial.

## Disclosure of Documents

Disclosure involves the listing by one party for the other of the *existence* of all essential documents which each party has in its custody, possession or control. This is done by way of "a list of documents". This will then be followed by the *inspection* by the other party's solicitor of those documents. The definition of documents is very wide and includes electronic documents, emails and word processed documents as well as more traditional "documents" such as letters, contracts and medical records. If both parties can see the evidence, it may help the parties to reach a settlement without the need for a trial.

However, disclosure of documents is no longer automatic. The parties or the court may decide that the documents are not the key to the case or that the essential ones have already been exchanged before proceedings began and so no specific disclosure step is necessary.

In most cases, the court will order "standard disclosure" of the documents on which each party is relying or which "adversely affect" that party's case or support the other's. Parties have a duty to search for the documents and have to provide a signed "disclosure statement" in their list of documents, stating what searches have and have not been carried out and the reasons why.

This test for disclosing documents is much narrower than the test which applied before the Civil Procedure Rules came into force. This required *all* documents which might have some bearing on the case to be disclosed and led to very large quantities of paper changing hands in some cases, even if none of them needed to be referred to at the trial. The aim of the new test is to cut down on the paperwork, time and costs.

However, if "standard disclosure" does not provide all the necessary information or one party is concerned that the other has not "searched" enough, the court can order additional "specific" disclosure or that a "further search" should be made, provided that the amount in dispute and the work involved justify this.

Sometimes experts may need to advise about disclosure of documents – what might exist and be necessary/helpful. Also, experts may need to see the other party's documents before preparing their report, but they should check with the solicitor which documents they have seen can/should be referred to in the report, in case any are "privileged", e.g letters between the client and solicitor, because once referred to that privilege may be "waived", i.e. given away.

### Witness Statements

Statements of witnesses of fact are also exchanged early in court proceedings, usually shortly after disclosure of documents. The solicitor will need to decide which of the statements the expert needs to see.

### Work with the Lawyers during Disclosure

It may be that after disclosure of documents and witness statements, the expert witness alters his or her opinion. The expert must communicate this to their instructing solicitors. Equally, it is very important that any new materials are passed on to the expert by the solicitors. A further report may be needed.

### Disclosure of Experts' Reports

This is covered in more detail in Chapter 2 but usually, when each side has their own expert, the two reports will be exchanged after disclosure of documents and witness statements. The new rules allow for questions to be put on the reports and for the experts to discuss or meet before trial to encourage settlement generally, or at least to narrow the areas of disagreement between the experts so that perhaps they may not have to attend at court (as this can add greatly to the costs of the case).

## SETTLEMENT

This is where the two parties to a dispute reach an agreement without the need for the case to proceed to a court hearing or further steps in the litigation process. The vast majority (about 96%) of civil cases settle before trial. It is in the interests of both parties to reach a settlement rather than to have to spend time and money on a trial. Sometimes the matter may be settled prior to litigation starting as a result of the information in the letter of claim or response, pre-action disclosure of documents or other information, or by negotiations or an ADR process. Experts may be asked to advise on settlement at this stage.

There are many other opportunities to reach a settlement as the litigation progresses. The court has a new power to "stay" proceedings after the defence is filed to give the parties an opportunity to try to settle.

It is often possible to settle cases after exchange of the evidence. Each side can then assess more objectively the relative strengths and weaknesses of their case. The expert may have a role in the settlement process. Where each side has retained an expert, an expert's report which identifies all the strengths of a case and is able to deal effectively with any areas of weakness may be an essential tool in reaching settlement.

Alternatively, where a single expert has been instructed by both parties, and one report covers the strengths and weaknesses of both parties' cases, the parties may find it easier to reach a compromise or one party may decide not to go ahead.

Under the previous rules of court, the defendant could try to settle a claim by paying money into court, based on what they thought the claim was worth. If the claimant accepted the amount, the case including the costs would be settled. If the claimant did not accept the amount and the action went on to trial, the judge would not be told about the payment but if he/she awarded the claimant more than the payment, the claimant would win and be awarded their costs. However, if the judgment was for less than the payment, the claimant would usually have to pay both sides' legal costs from the date of the payment. This was a powerful weapon for defendants.

Now the claimants have a similar tool. Under the rules, either party can make an **"offer to settle"** at any time, including before proceedings begin. By a recent amendment to the rules, defendants no longer have to substantiate their offer to settle by making a payment into court of the sum offered. However, if the claimant accepts the offer, the sum must be paid within 14 days or the defendant will lose the cost benefits of the rule.

If the defendant does not accept the claimant's offer:

- If the judge awards the claimant less, they will not usually receive their costs from the date when the time for accepting the offer expired.

- If the judge awards the claimant more, the defendant will usually be ordered to pay additional interest on the claimant's damages (up to 10%), and *all* the claimant's costs on the most generous (indemnity) basis, with interest.

These rules encourage both parties to take a realistic view of their case, especially if the other side makes an offer, and have led to more cases settling without a trial.

Experts, especially those advising on the value of a claim, may be asked to advise more often than in the past on settlement offers.

## THE LATER STAGES OF AN ACTION

If a case has not settled after the evidence has been exchanged, the court will send the parties a **"listing questionnaire"** to complete about 10 weeks before the trial is due to take place. This will act as a check on whether the parties have complied with the previous court directions and are ready for trial. The court will fix a definite trial date, if this has not already been done (taking into account the key players' availability but only within reason) and may in more complex or difficult cases call the parties and their lawyers into a "pre-trial review" to plan the trial itself, including whether any experts will have to attend to give oral evidence.

The court may also ask the parties to prepare additional information for the trial judge, including:

- A chronology of events.

- A short statement of the disputed issues.

- "Skeleton arguments" – a note of the main points to be covered by the advocates at the trial.

- In technical or complex cases, a reading guide to the main documents for the judge.

Experts may be asked to assist, especially in the preparation of the reading guide, and they may be involved in discussions or meetings at this stage to assist with a settlement or, in any event, to narrow the issues in dispute.

## PROCEDURE OF A CIVIL TRIAL

1. The claimant's advocate makes a short opening speech. He or she explains the facts to the judge and sets out the issues in dispute.

2. Sometimes, the defence may make an opening speech.

3. The claimant's witnesses give evidence. Usually their witness statement is "taken as read" and stands as evidence in chief. The witness is cross-examined by the defendant's lawyer. The witness may be re-examined by the claimant's advocate but only if anything new has come up in the cross-examination which requires clarification.

4. The defendant's witnesses give evidence, in the same way as the claimant's witnesses.

5. Closing speeches: the defendant's lawyer goes first, followed by the claimant's lawyer.

Note that exchange of documents, witness of fact statements and expert reports means that each party will know in advance what oral evidence the witnesses are likely to give. Note also that it is the evidence taken as read or given in the witness box which the judge takes into account when reaching a decision.

In many trials today, and especially Fast Track trials, the court will set time limits in advance for each party's evidence. Trials that last longer than necessary greatly increase the costs of the litigation and inconvenience other cases and the court's management of its resources.

## EVIDENCE IN CIVIL TRIALS

Evidence in civil trials, like that in criminal trials, can be divided into three categories: documentary evidence, real evidence and witness evidence.

Documentary evidence includes photographs, video recordings and tape recordings, as well as documents (such as letters, internal memoranda, hospital notes and e-mails and computer records) made by the parties themselves during the period which is the focus of the action.

Real evidence is any material object produced to the court for inspection. This may include anything from the weapon in a trial of trespass to the person, to the automatic recording of radar traces showing the position of a ship in an Admiralty action. Confusingly, photographs, video recordings and tape recordings may be both "documents" and real evidence.

With regard to witnesses, once again there are three types: witnesses of fact, expert witnesses and professional witnesses.

## WITNESSES OF FACT

A witness of fact in a civil trial is someone who is called to give evidence in a case about what happened. They are there to recall what they saw, heard or did. They are not generally allowed to give opinion evidence. Contrast this with an expert witness who may give both factual and opinion evidence.

There are many kinds of witnesses of fact in civil cases, such as a witness who saw a car accident in which the claimant was injured; a witness who recalls the medical advice given to a patient who has a claim for clinical professional negligence; and a witness who recorded the results of a scientific experiment.

A witness of fact will often give oral evidence at trial. This is because oral evidence is deemed to be the best form of evidence as it can be tested under cross-examination.

Witnesses giving oral evidence in the witness box may refresh their memory from any contemporaneous notes they may have kept. Contemporaneous notes are records completed while the facts were still fresh in the witness's mind. Such a contemporaneous note is part of the oral evidence and may be read out by the witness. The other party has the right to request and inspect such notes.

Examples of such notes are a police officer's notebook, a piece of paper on which a passer-by has written down the registration number of a car involved in an accident, records of scientific experiments, records of an audit carried out by accountants and medical records.

Where professional persons are to give factual evidence, it is important for them to keep accurate and full notes. The following information is important:

- Dates, time, location.

- Who was present (patient, client, researchers).

- Examinations/experiments and findings.

- Details of observed facts and, if an expert, his/her opinion on the facts.

- Details of conversations/advice given.

### Witness Statements in Civil Trials

Witnesses of fact write statements, not reports. A statement will often be written some time after the events it records. It will usually be written at the request of one of the parties or their solicitor. The purpose of such a statement is to set out in writing the details of a particular event or series of events as far as possible in the witness's own words. Parties do not "own" witnesses of fact – either party can ask an eyewitness to give a statement and sometimes both parties do so! All witness statements must include a signed statement of truth.

The Civil Procedure Rules give the court powers to control the number of witnesses of fact whose statements are disclosed and/or who give evidence at the trial. The court will issue directions after allocating the case to a track. Usually witness statements are exchanged after documents are disclosed but before experts' reports are exchanged.

Increasingly, at trial the written statements "stand as evidence" and take the place of examination in chief (questions asked by the lawyer of the party who calls the witness). Further, if the statement is not controversial and the other side does not wish to cross-examine the witness about it, the statement may be taken as read without the necessity of the witness attending.

A witness statement is always available for the witness to refresh his or her memory before going into the witness box to give evidence. If the witness has contemporaneous notes, then those can be taken into the witness box.

## EXPERT WITNESSES

An expert witness may give evidence of both fact and opinion.

Facts fall into two different categories. Firstly, there are facts that experts have observed for themselves, for example the crack in the floor of a building, an X-ray or the accounts of one of the parties.

Secondly, there are facts that an expert has been told by someone else, for example the date on which a floor of a building was completed, the amount of pain being suffered by a patient or the reason why certain items in the accounts have been described as extraordinary items. This category will include facts that have been reported to an expert by a member of his/her team of researchers or auditors (these people may be called as witnesses too).

Experts must take great care to identify the source of the facts on which they base their expert opinion. Facts which an expert has observed first-hand will usually be given greater weight than facts that the expert has been told by another person. The veracity of facts reported to an expert by another person may be tested at trial by the cross-examination of the person who supplied those facts to the expert. For example, a claimant in a personal injury case may be cross-examined about whether he really was suffering from the level of pain about which he told his expert surgeon. It may be suggested in cross-examination that the claimant was exaggerating his condition.

Expert opinion evidence is admissible in court on matters not within the common knowledge of the court, but only with the express permission of the court. Opinion evidence can be based upon experiment, experience, research or the work of others. Experts are invited to give such opinion evidence because of their qualifications and experience in their field of expertise.

It has already been seen that any expert's report which is to be relied upon at trial must be disclosed to the other party well before the trial. If the experts on both sides agree with one another, their reports may be read at trial without the need for either of them to attend.

In more complicated cases, the experts may have a discussion or meeting prior to trial. The aim of this meeting will be to iron out differences and to identify those issues on which agreement cannot be reached. At trial, cross-examination will focus on these areas of disagreement.

### Opinion on Liability and Quantum

In most civil cases, the judge will make the decision on liability and quantum. However, the judge may be helped by hearing the opinion of expert witnesses. For example, a forensic accountant may be asked to assess the amount of money a claimant has lost by reason of the injuries which the claimant sustained in a road traffic accident.

## PROFESSIONAL WITNESSES

Most professional witnesses give evidence as a result of seeing or doing something in the course of their everyday job. Giving evidence will be a part of their job. Good examples of professional witnesses are police officers and police surgeons. Professional witnesses give mainly factual evidence but can give opinion evidence based on their qualifications and experience. Their evidence is given in the form of a statement and not a report. This statement may be read out in court without the need for them to give oral evidence. However, the other party may ask for them to be called to give evidence and to be cross-examined.

## WITNESS ATTENDANCE

It is usual for solicitors to ask the witnesses from whom they have taken statements whether they will attend court voluntarily. If a witness refuses to reply to the solicitor's enquiry or indicates that they will not attend voluntarily, then the solicitor will get the court to make an order that the witness attends. The witness will be served with a witness summons. If the witness then fails to attend, they may be arrested and fined and/or imprisoned for contempt of court. When a witness is served with a witness summons, the witness must be offered a sum to cover their travelling expenses to and from court and a sum to compensate them for their loss of time which may be incurred by attending court. The rate for this is fixed by the Crown Court. It is common for expert witnesses to charge a fee for attending court.

Certain categories of witnesses (such as police officers) will often ask the solicitor to arrange for them to be served with a witness summons because they need such a document in order to prove to their employer that they are required to have time off work to attend a civil trial!

# Chapter 2

# THE ROLE OF THE EXPERT

## SUMMARY

- The need for experts •
- The changing role of experts in civil cases •
- The differences between lawyers and expert witnesses •
- What lawyers require from experts •
- Taking instructions from lawyers •
- Meetings with other experts •
- Applying to the court for directions in civil cases •
- Professional negligence and breach of contract •

## THE NEED FOR EXPERTS

Experts are individuals with qualifications and experience which enable them to give opinions on the facts of, issues in or likely value of, cases within their specialist field. When providing evidence for the court they are independent of the case although they may be instructed and paid by only one of the parties. Their role is to help the parties, the lawyers and particularly the court to understand technical matters in the case.

Their evidence for the court may be in two forms, a written report and oral evidence given in the witness box.

The main functions of an expert can be described as follows:

1. To act as an adviser to one party only and to provide *preliminary advice and/or a report* to help the party and their solicitor decide

whether there is a case and, if so, what the strengths and weaknesses are. (See Chapter 1.)

2. To act as an expert witness for, or in, court proceedings to help the court in resolving the dispute. This may include providing a *written report* (for both parties and the court, when jointly instructed, or for one party initially and for exchange with the other party's like expert's report, and for disclosure to the court when each party has their own expert) and giving oral evidence at trial from the witness box when the court requires this. (See Chapter 3.)

Other functions might include:

3. To help in drafting legal documents needed for the court.

4. To advise on documents for, or provided, during disclosure of documents.

5. To comment on, or to help prepare questions on the other party's expert's report.

6. To meet with other experts to try to narrow the areas of disagreement.

7. To advise on negotiating a settlement.

8. To sit with the judge and act as an assessor at a trial.

## THE CHANGING ROLE OF EXPERTS IN CIVIL CASES FOLLOWING THE IMPLEMENTATION OF LORD WOOLF'S CIVIL JUSTICE REFORMS

During Lord Woolf's *Access to Justice* enquiry, he became particularly concerned that parties in civil claims too often introduced expert evidence which was not necessary and, sometimes, which was too specifically tailored to support that party's case. He concluded that the over-reliance on "partisan" one-sided expert evidence was a significant factor in the delays and rising costs of much litigation and could, on occasions, hinder or delay a settlement.

Accordingly, the Civil Procedure Rules give the courts, through the judges' case management powers, considerable control over when expert evidence can be introduced, both in terms of numbers and types of experts, in what form and at what stage, and how much of the experts' fees the winning party might recover from the losing party.

The Civil Procedure Rules stress that the expert's "overriding" duty is to the court, not to the party who instructs or pays the expert.

The rules require the parties to try, whenever possible, to "share" an expert by jointly instructing one person from a particular discipline rather than one each, especially in Small Claims and Fast Track cases; the court has the power to order joint instructions if the parties do not co-operate.

Evidence collated for a report into the operation of the Civil Procedure Rules (*The Management of Civil Cases: The Courts and Post-Woolf Landscape*, DCA Research Series 9/05, November 2005) suggests that the pre-action protocols (in particular, the personal injury protocol) and the courts in lower-value cases or where only "technical" matters or quantum are at issue, single experts are being used increasingly. The court will rarely appoint the single expert – the judge will instead encourage the parties to work together to select and instruct a suitable person.

The rules also set out very specific requirements for the contents of experts' reports (see Chapter 3).

The courts are already making it very clear that the judges and not the parties, lawyers or experts are in control when it comes to expert evidence. For instance, in *Rollinson v Kimberly Clark* (1999) 15 June CA, it was said that it was not acceptable for a solicitor to try to instruct an expert shortly before trial without checking the experts' availability because court dates cannot be changed simply to suit an expert's convenience. In *British Sugar Plc v Cegelec Ltd* [2004] EWCA Civ 1450, the defendant was not allowed to rely on expert evidence because he had applied for permission to do so after the trial had commenced, and this would have necessitated an adjournment. The defendant argued that it was in the interests of justice for this evidence to be admitted. The Court of Appeal held that the first instance judge was entitled to refuse the defendant permission to rely on this evidence. The message from the civil courts to experts is that "you must fit in with the court's requirements, given the court's scarce resources". You have been warned!

The paramount concern for the courts is whether the evidence is required to enable the court to deal with case "justly" as required by CPR Part 1.1 (the overriding objective) but also to ensure that the parties are on an equal footing (CPR Part 1.1(2)). In exceptional circumstances, therefore, the court may allow more than one expert from the same discipline to be called (see *ES v Chesterfield and North Derbyshire Royal Hospital NHS Trust* [2003] EWCA Civ 1284).

Other ways in which the court might to seek to economise on expert evidence and encourage greater co-operation include:

- Ordering that expert evidence is not needed at all, e.g. where the judge should be able to decide the issues based on the factual evidence.

- Ordering that expert evidence will be by written report only – no oral evidence – especially in Small Claims and Fast Track cases.

- Requiring one expert to co-ordinate the work of others from different disciplines into one comprehensive report.

- Varying the usual arrangement that expert reports are exchanged simultaneously – if one party discloses first, the second party might decide he/she does not need an expert at all.

- Allowing parties to put written questions to experts on their reports – the Rules provide that these should be for clarification only and must be put, once only, within 28 days of service of the report.

- Ordering the experts to meet or hold a discussion before trial and produce an agreed note of the meeting.

- Placing a limit on the amount of experts' fees which can be recovered by the winning party.

## THE ROLE OF THE EXPERT: TO GIVE OPINION EVIDENCE

The role of the expert witness is commonly misunderstood.

An expert witness may be needed to give clear, independent opinion evidence on the subject within his or her field. This field is defined by reference to the expert's qualifications and experience. An expert should not give opinion evidence outside his or her field of expertise and should not accept the role in cases outside their expertise.

An expert's role is thus as an educator, in the first instance to assist the party and their lawyers in the preparation of the case, which may include providing some written advice; and, secondly, if the case goes to court to prepare a report for the court and sometimes to give oral evidence at trial, to assist the judge to reach a fair decision. Sometimes two different experts will be asked to fill these two different roles – one to advise, perhaps "behind the scenes", and the second to be the court expert witness, perhaps on joint instructions with the other party.

Lord Woolf made it abundantly clear that experts are not "hired guns". Their role is not to win the case. The lawyers are the advocates who present their clients' arguments; the expert is a witness giving evidence of his or her opinion, based on his or her knowledge and experience. Experts must avoid biased, exaggerated evidence.

Expert witness evidence is often very important. It must be based on a sound foundation of facts which have been properly and vigorously investigated. Acquiring these facts may involve such activities as examining a patient, asking a patient questions, conducting an experiment or visiting the site of a building which has structural problems. Experts should always be prepared to explain why they reached their expert opinion given a certain set of facts.

## THE ROLE OF THE LAWYER: TO REPRESENT THE PARTY

Lawyers represent their client's case in court. They are paid to win but do have a professional duty to assist the court. The lawyers have to do the best they can with the available evidence. They have a discretion in deciding which evidence to use and how to present it, subject to the court's control, and will marshal it in a way that is most favourable to their client's case. However, lawyers must not knowingly present false evidence and have a duty not to positively mislead the court. For example, they must not knowingly withhold relevant evidence from witnesses or allow a witness to tell lies in the witness box.

The lawyers *do not give evidence* – they are not witnesses. Their role is to argue and seek to persuade the judge to decide in favour of their client.

## DIFFERENCES BETWEEN AN EXPERT WITNESS AND A LAWYER

| *Expert Witness* | *Lawyer* |
| --- | --- |
| Independent | Partisan |
| Neutral | Puts client's case |
| Knows about field, not law | Knows about law, not field |
| Witness | Advocate |
| Gives evidence | Represents the client |
| Never argues | Argues |

| | |
|---|---|
| Assists the judge | Persuades the judge |
| Not a hired gun | Paid by the client |

## WHAT THE INSTRUCTING LAWYERS REQUIRE FROM AN EXPERT

It is important to understand what the lawyers require.

When an expert is to be engaged, the lawyers will want to make sure that the expert is the right person for the case. In an initial meeting or telephone call with the lawyers, an expert should expect to be asked probing questions, for example about qualifications and experience, whether the expert usually acts for claimants or defendants, or whether the expert has had previous court experience. The expert's "track record" may be even more important when the instructions are to act jointly for both parties. The lawyers will listen to the responses and note the level of confidence, the clarity of expression and the expert's overall honesty and integrity.

It is important that you draw to the solicitor's attention any potential conflict of interest so that the solicitor can decide whether to proceed with your instructions. There is no specific requirement in the Civil Procedure Rules or the Protocol on this point but the Court of Appeal in *Toth v Jarman* [2006] EWCA Civ 1028 suggested that the Civil Procedure Rules Committee should consider adding a statement of conflicts to the required contents of the expert's report. The expert's curriculum vitae should be appended to your report and should include details of any activity or employment which might give rise to a conflict. If the other side challenge this and the matter cannot be resolved, it will be for the court to decide whether a conflict of interest should prevent the expert from acting.

An expert who is defensive, confused, verbose or obviously partisan to, e.g. accident victims or insurers, is likely to be avoided by lawyers.

Do not be intimidated by a lack of previous court experience. It is expertise in a particular field that is most important.

An expert may occasionally be asked by the client, solicitors or barristers to modify or change aspects of a report, or on rare occasions even their opinion, to help win the case. However, the expert should bear in mind the words of Lord Wilberforce in *Whitehouse v Jordan* ([1981] 1 WLR 246 at page 256):

"It is necessary that expert evidence presented to the court should be, and should be seen to be, the independent product of the expert, uninfluenced as to form or content by the exigences of litigation. To the extent that it is not, the evidence is likely to be not only incorrect but self-defeating."

The importance of the independence of the expert witness and his/her duty to the court is reiterated in paragraph 4 of the Protocol for the Instruction of Experts to give Evidence in Civil Claims (Annex to the Practice Direction to CPR Part 35) (Appendix 4).

Remember that the expert's professional credibility is on the line if the lawyer persuades him or her to exaggerate the true position in terms of their expert opinion.

## TAKING INSTRUCTIONS: WHAT THE EXPERT NEEDS TO KNOW

- Are you the right expert for the job? Be clear on what the lawyer and client need expertise in. A general practitioner should not profess to be an expert in open heart surgery!

- Are you being instructed by one party only or by both? If the latter, will you receive one letter of instruction or two?

- Does the client/lawyer want preliminary advice (to see if there is a case for the claimant to bring or the defendant to defend), a report for disclosure to the other side and to the court, or ultimately both?

- What do the lawyers want you to do – to look at liability, causation or quantum (see Chapter 1)?

- What are the deadlines/time limits for providing advice or writing a report? Are these court imposed? Can you definitely comply? If you have doubts you should not accept the work.

- How much will you be paid and when (see Chapter 5 on fees)?

- What are the terms and conditions for you providing your expert service (see Chapter 3)?

- Have proceedings started yet? Has the claim form been issued and in which court (see Chapter 1)?

- If proceedings have started, at what stage are they? Has the case been allocated to a track? Has the court issued any directions, especially with regard to expert evidence, or set a trial date?

- Are there any court documents which you need to see? For example, the particulars of claim and the defence/counterclaim. These can be very helpful as they should set out the main issues in the case.

- Are there any witness statements? Can you see them?

- Are there any reports from experts instructed by other parties to the proceedings? Can you see them? Does the identity of these experts put you in any difficulties, e.g. a close colleague?

- Are there any other experts instructed by the client/solicitor instructing you? What are their areas of expertise? What are their findings and opinions?

- Do you have copies of all essential documents, e.g. medical records, photographs, diagrams, etc.? Are any of these privileged? If so, should you see them or send them back?

- Do you need permission/consent to visit a site or examine a patient (especially if you are jointly instructed) and has this been obtained?

Do not be afraid to ask the lawyers if you do not understand what you are being asked to do.

Also, check carefully before you accept instructions whether you or your firm could be in a conflict of interest because you act for, or have acted for, the other party in the case.

Be proactive in getting more detailed instructions as you go along but remember you will need to summarise your instructions in any report you prepare for the court. Help to educate the client and the lawyers as to what the issues are. In complex technical areas, the expert is more likely to be able to see what the issues are than the client or the lawyers.

## Duty of Confidentiality to Instructing Solicitor's Client

Usually the expert is instructed and paid by the solicitors, not the client. The contract is between the solicitors and the expert. However, the established law is that communications between the expert and the solicitor cannot be disclosed without the *consent* of the solicitor's client. Likewise, expert reports cannot be disclosed to the other side unless the solicitor's client gives consent, except where they have been prepared on a joint basis for the two parties.

## How Legal Professional Privilege Affects the Expert Witness

The established law is that communications between solicitors and their client and communications between an expert and instructing solicitors are protected or privileged from being seen by anyone but the instructing solicitors and the client. This protection existed so long as what the expert was saying or writing was done for the purpose of giving advice in litigation and it came into existence after litigation was contemplated or commenced.

Prior to the introduction of the Civil Procedure Rules, instructions to experts were protected by privilege, as they fell within the category of communications between solicitors and third parties. However,

CPR Part 35.10(4) makes it clear that instructions to experts are no longer privileged and the substance of all material instructions (whether written or oral) must be set out in the report. Recent cases have confirmed that this rule is not intended to sweep away privilege generally in this area and that earlier draft reports will not be disclosable (*Jackson v Marley Davenport Ltd* [2004] EWCA Civ 1102). The court will not order disclosure of specific documents in relation to instructions or permit the expert to be questioned in court about them unless the court considers that the statement of instructions in the expert's report is inaccurate or incomplete.

## Changing Experts

In some cases, it may be necessary for the solicitors to instruct a different expert; because the original expert's area of expertise is not entirely appropriate for the case, for example. The solicitor may need permission from the court to change experts. Permission will certainly be required if the original expert was named in the case management directions. If permission is required, it is likely to be a requirement that the report of the first expert is disclosed (see *Beck v Ministry of Defence* [2004] EWCA Civ 1034 and *Hajigeorgiou v Vasiliou* [2005] EWCA Civ 2360). Caution is required even if the second report is obtained before proceedings are commenced (see *Carruthers v MP Fireworks Ltd and Balfour Convenience Stores Ltd* (unreported, Bristol County Court, 26th January 2007).

## COACHING

### Clients, Solicitors or Barristers Cannot Coach Witnesses

Expert witnesses are an important resource. Cases can be won or lost on the strength of the expert's opinion evidence. However, lawyers are bound by their own professional rules *not* to coach witnesses; that is, they cannot tell witnesses what they ought to say. The Bar Standards Board, which regulates barristers' conduct, has issued detailed guidance on this in the light of recent cases (see *R v Momodou* [2005] EWCA Crim 177 and *Ultraframe (UK) Ltd v Fielding and Others* [2005] EWHC (Ch)). (This is quite different from a solicitor explaining to a "novice" expert witness what is likely to happen in court, or a barrister or advocate trying out cross-examination questions in conference.) Witness familiarisation, designed to ensure that those who face court proceedings undergo a process of familiarisation to gain knowledge of the procedures involved and to enable them to give a correct account from the witness box, is acceptable but any training aimed at encouraging a witness to alter his/her evidence is unacceptable and puts the trainer in potential breach of their rules of professional conduct and might discredit the witness' evidence.

### Can Experts Coach Lawyers?

Yes, they can and should. One of the most important roles of an expert is to work with the lawyers to help to clarify and explain complex technical areas. Experts can also help the advocate to ask them the right questions during the trial and also to put the right questions to the experts called for the other party at trial.

## MEETINGS WITH OTHER EXPERTS

### The Purpose of Discussions or Meetings Between Experts

The purpose of a meeting between experts is twofold.

First to discuss technical matters within their expertise and second to discuss their respective opinions on these technical matters.

It is important for expert witnesses to have a frank discussion of the strengths and weaknesses of the technical aspects of the case. These discussions enable the experts to pool the relevant technical information, to highlight areas where further investigation is required and prevent significant matters being overlooked. A greater understanding of the issues can be acquired as well as a greater understanding of the reasons for the other expert's opinion. If the reports have not yet been written, this will help the experts to write shorter, clearer and more relevant reports.

Where the court has ordered a discussion or meeting to take place, the experts must produce a joint statement of matters that are agreed and those that are still in dispute. Such agreements between the experts are not binding on the parties or the court; but the court is likely to order that the note should be placed on the court file.

## Court Orders for Discussions or Meetings Prior to Trial

In civil proceedings the court may *order* a meeting and the Civil Procedure Rules specifically encourage the court to do so. In lower value, Fast Track and similar cases, the "meeting" might take place by telephone to keep costs in proportion. The court may define the object of the meeting and give the experts authority to discuss those matters, or this may be left to the parties and their lawyers. Setting a clear agenda and timetable in advance will be vital.

An expert does not have the power to reach a binding agreement with another expert during these meetings, since the expert does not represent the party but is an independent witness. However, the parties may expressly agree to be bound by what is agreed at the meeting and, if they do not agree to this, they must be able to explain their refusal to the court since this will have an impact on the overall costs of the case.

Lawyers and the parties usually will not be present during court ordered meetings. However, the lawyers can use the results to negotiate a settlement.

## Meeting Agreed Between the Parties

The parties may *agree* to a "without prejudice" meeting of experts at any time before proceedings have started or during the litigation or even during the trial. The parties themselves always define the object of such a meeting and the lawyers and the parties may be present. The experts can be given varying degrees of authority from being allowed to settle very little to reaching agreement on technical matters. An expert must be clear on what are the main issues in dispute before the meeting takes place.

*Preparation for Meetings*

Preparation for *any* meeting with other experts is very important. The lawyers must help with identifying the main issues and setting the agenda. It is helpful if the lawyers draft a list of questions which the experts should answer. The experts should draw up a joint document at the end of the meeting and sign it. This will list under headings areas of agreement or disagreement and give the experts' reasons.

## APPLYING TO THE COURT FOR DIRECTIONS

In civil cases, experts have a right to apply directly to the court for directions, in recognition of their role during litigation, to help the court, not just the party who instructs them. This power might be used when the expert:

- Has conflicting instructions from the parties when acting as a single expert.

- Knows or suspects one of the parties is keeping back information from him/her or is acting fraudulently.

- Feels strongly that an issue which neither party has raised may be vital to the case.

- Is experiencing difficulties dealing with the questions raised by any of the parties under CPR Part 35.6.

However, it is a power to be used sparingly because clearly the expert will not be popular with solicitors if he/she "runs to the court" too often with minor problems.

## PROFESSIONAL NEGLIGENCE AND BREACH OF CONTRACT

Experts must appreciate the responsibility they have for their advice. An expert is responsible for carrying out a full and thorough investigation into the facts. The client and lawyers will often rely on the expert to study documents and carry out experiments and research to find out all the available information.

The views which an expert gives in an advice or preliminary report are their work, not the lawyers'. If the expert has carried out insufficient investigations, does not have enough information to form an opinion or has become too partisan in their opinion, he or she may later be found to be negligent, in breach of contract or possibly subject to disciplinary action. The main pitfalls for experts are:

- Inadequate instructions – the instructions do not cover all the issues. However, the expert has a responsibility to look beyond the instructions given.

- Failure to give independent/impartial advice. Remember, it is the *expert's* opinion not the lawyer's. An expert can be sued for giving an opinion that no reasonable expert in that field of expertise could come to. *The expert must give bona fide independent expert opinion.* Would the expert express the same opinion if the instructions had come from the opposing party?

- Failure of communication between the solicitor's client and the expert. Take full statements in writing from the client or make sure these are provided.

- Failure to agree in writing what service the expert is providing. There may be an expectation gap between the service given and the service expected. The expert should be clear as to what (s)he is giving expert advice on and what the purpose of this advice is.

- Breach of confidentiality by expert or defamation of someone in the advice.

- Technical errors. An example is an expert who was found to be negligent because he grossly over-valued the potential damages the claimant would be awarded at trial. The claimant, on the basis of this information, did not accept an early payment into court by the defendant. Later the claimant was awarded damages of significantly less. (A payment into court is where one party gives money to the court to be given to the other party. The other party can withdraw that money and end the case. If they do not, then they are liable for all the legal costs of the case from then on if the judge orders a lesser sum to be paid at the trial.)

- Failure to acknowledge other possibilities. Consider if it is appropriate to say "If A happened, then.....; if B, then.....". This will show an awareness of different factors and also indicate an unwillingness to conceal information.

### How to Avoid Claims of Professional Negligence/Breach of Contract

1. The expert must be able to prove that (s)he did a good job and exercised reasonable care and skill to avoid a successful claim of professional negligence. The expert must keep good notes of what (s)he did and set out all of the facts and instructions that were material to the opinion in the report (see *R v Bowman* [2006] EWCA Crim 417).

2. Keep up-to-date through training/research, etc.

3. Be clear in the advice given and keep the lawyers informed.

4. Ask for more information and indicate if you have insufficient factual evidence on which to base an opinion.

5. If a draft report is provided, indicate what information was known at the time and what further information is needed and/or requested.

6. Do not be tempted to provide an opinion on an issue that falls outside your area of expertise.

7. After the experts' meeting, do not make any subsequent concessions unless instructed to do so.

8. Never be tempted to fabricate any evidence or assume any facts without checking their accuracy.

9. Always tell the truth.

*Key Contents of Good Notes*

- Basic information such as dates, time, location.

- Who else was present, e.g. other employees, a patient, the solicitor's client, a police officer.

- If consent was to be obtained, how was this done?

- What was the purpose of an examination, site visit or experiment?

- The findings of the examination or investigation.

- Detailed observation of *facts* and *opinions*.

- Details of any follow-up inspection or examination.

It is important to note that it may be several years before you personally, or your company, are sued for negligence or you have to give evidence as an expert witness. You *must* be able to verify what actually happened and why.

Consider a consultant gynaecologist who delivers hundreds of babies each year. Three years after the delivery of a particular child, he/she has a claim of professional negligence brought against him/her. The court will not be impressed with "memory" only. In cross-examination that consultant will be pulled to pieces unless there is some concrete evidence of what actually happened.

Keep your notes for at least six years (as breach of contract cases can be brought for up to six years after the breach is discovered. Negligence cases can be brought up to three years after the negligent act).

## Protection from Claims When Acting as a Court Expert Witness

Professionals may be found negligent for actions/decisions when working in their professional capacity and when advising a party at the early stages of a claim or outside legal proceedings. Generally, however, expert witnesses in legal proceedings, whose main role is to assist the court, have protection from negligence suits in a similar way to barristers and other advocates. Nevertheless, bear in mind that if the judge considers that an act or omission in the way an expert witness has carried out his duties indicates that he is not fit to practise his discipline and/or what he has done amounts to professional misconduct, the judge may refer the expert to his disciplinary body (see *General Medical Council v Meadow* [2006] EWCA Civ 1390).

## Professional Indemnity Insurance

No matter how careful or experienced an expert is in a field, it is possible to make mistakes. It is imperative to have professional indemnity insurance. These insurance policies not only pay damages but can also help with payment of the legal costs of any investigation, settlement or defence work.

Professional indemnity insurers have access to expert lawyers and loss adjusters to give expert witnesses the best possible defence.

# WRITING REPORTS

## WHAT IS THE PURPOSE OF A REPORT?

A report is written by an expert to help the parties in the preparation of the case and/or to help the court to reach a decision. The report is for people who are not experts in the specialist field that the report is about. The report, whether for the client or for the court, must contain details of all the facts which the expert has relied on to reach his or her opinion, which should be a reasoned analysis of the strengths and weaknesses of the case.

The facts and opinions should be tailored to address the key issues in the case that the instructions have established. For example, in a professional negligence claim, the issues may be 1) that the professional person was acting in a situation where a duty of care to the client was owed; 2) that there was a breach of this duty, i.e. no reasonable professional person would have acted in that way; and 3) that the breach caused the damage/injury.

In an advisory report to the client, the expert should try as far as possible to anticipate all the arguments that may be put forward by the other party's expert. These arguments should be addressed and any weaknesses pointed out.

In a report for disclosure to the other party and to the court, the expert has a duty to remain independent and to express his/her objective opinion but only on issues which are within his/her expertise and which are part of the dispute before the court, as presented in the evidence. The expert's duty does not extend to raising matters which are outside the issues being put before the court. There may be rare occasions in a civil claim when the expert considers that not to raise a particular matter might mislead the court and in such a case the expert might want to make use of their power to apply to the court for directions.

Where each party has their own expert, the expert should be aiming to persuade the judge/jury that his/her expert opinion is to be preferred to the other expert's opinion as it has more strengths.

## HOW THE REPORT WILL BE USED IN COURT

At trial, the expert may be called to give oral evidence and be cross-examined in the witness box. This will be rare in civil Fast Track cases, and in some larger Multi Track actions the expert may be called to give oral evidence but the report will be taken as read and he/she will go straight into cross-examination.

In criminal trials, the report may be in the form of a section 9 statement. This means that it has been served on the other party and the other party does not object to it being read in court instead of calling the witness to give oral evidence. If the other party objects to the section 9 statement, then the witness will have to give oral evidence and be cross-examined.

There is also an opportunity in civil trials for the parties to agree that the expert's report can be used as evidence without calling the expert to give oral evidence.

The judge in civil cases, and the judge and jury in criminal cases, will have a copy of the expert report if it is admissible and the expert himself may not be called as a witness. Where the witness is giving oral evidence, the report makes it easier for them to follow the evidence. The expert witness should use the report to help explain points to the judge and/or jury.

## AGREE TERMS AND CONDITIONS BEFORE WRITING THE REPORT

The contract for services is usually between the expert and the instructing solicitors, not between the solicitors' client and the expert. If the solicitors are not paid by their client, they are still obliged to pay the expert.

You should have a standard pro forma letter to send out on receiving instructions, setting out your terms and conditions. The following matters should be covered:

1. *Set out what you understand are the services you are expected to perform.*

   Preparation of preliminary advice and/or court report, attendance at meetings, attendance at conference with counsel, attendance at court, etc. It is important to be clear on this. A gap between what you think you are to do and what the solicitors think they have asked you to do can give rise to negligence claims or complaints and/or no further work.

2. *Set out the obligations of the instructing client or solicitors.*

   Detail the documents you need to be provided with, e.g. the claimant's statement, relevant medical records relating to the claimant, the claimant's statement of case, the defence and counterclaim, reports of other experts, advice from counsel, all relevant documents, other witness statements, etc.

3. *Set out the obligations that you have as the expert.*

That you will use reasonable skill and care in the performance of instructions given to you, preserve the confidentiality of information/ documents/correspondence relating to the case.

4. *Timing.*

Set out when the report will be delivered.

5. *Fees.*

Indicate how these will be charged – a flat fee or an hourly rate based on the amount of time involved, travelling expenses, cancellation charges, fees for attending court and the time for making payment. Will you charge interest on outstanding invoices?

See Appendix 1 for a specimen pro forma on terms and conditions.

It is very important that the issue of fees is addressed at this stage. As only about 4% of cases actually get to court (the rest being settled beforehand), most experts invoice the solicitors after the report has been written. Even if the case is to go to trial, a preliminary invoice for the writing of the report may be sent.

The payment of experts' fees is dealt with fully in Chapter 5.

## WRITING AN EXCELLENT EXPERT REPORT

Expert evidence in court takes two forms: the expert's written report and their oral evidence. However, as some 96% of civil cases settle without going to court, the majority of cases are settled on the basis of the written evidence in the form of the expert's report.

An excellent report can influence the client, the solicitors who instruct you, the advocates giving advice to your party and the other party's expert, solicitors and advocates. If the case goes to trial, the report must be able to influence the person who decides the case – the judge, the jury or the magistrates.

You are completely in control of the written evidence in your report. If you are called to give oral evidence at court, you will gain a lot of confidence by having an excellent report to which you can refer to help explain the case and your opinion. A good report often forms the core document in the case.

The purpose of a report is to provide *information* for the parties to the case and, if the case goes to trial, for the judge. The information must be set out in a succinct, clear, easy to read style. Remember that the report is to be read by people who are not experts in your field. Imagine the judge using your report as a pair of spectacles to look at the evidence so it comes into sharp focus.

Report writing is a two stage process: first gathering factual information by interviewing witnesses, visiting the scene, carrying out detailed research and investigations, etc. and secondly coming to your expert opinion on those facts.

## Get Clear Instructions for Writing Your Report

Make sure the instructions you receive are as clear as possible and do not make any unnecessary assumptions. Before you start your investigations and research, find out what you are supposed to be doing.

Discuss the issues with the solicitors until you are both happy with what you are supposed to be looking at. Good instructions will ensure you write an excellent report.

Solicitors may not always give you as clear instructions as you need. They may simply send you a letter saying "Please do a report" without telling you in sufficient detail what the case is about, how far it has reached and whether you are acting for one party or both.

Ask the solicitors for what you need. You may be able to do this in simple cases by sending them a pro forma letter which asks who the parties are, what the facts are, how long you have to write the report, the amount you will be paid per hour/per report. In criminal cases, ask what the charge is and what the defence is. In civil cases, ask why one party is suing another.

In more complex cases you may need to speak to the solicitors a number of times. If you do not understand what you are supposed to be doing or what the issues are, then do not be afraid to ask until you do understand. Be proactive, remember you are the expert – you know what you need. You also need to be clear about fees from the outset (see Chapter 5 and pro forma letter in Appendix 1).

## What is the Purpose of this Particular Report?

You may be doing a preliminary advisory report, that is a report to be used by the client and solicitors to decide if the case is worth pursuing or defending.

You may be doing a report to assist in drafting the formal court documents (statements of case).

You may be doing a report for one of the parties which will be disclosed to both parties during the proceedings and which may be used to settle the case or at trial.

You may be doing a report for both parties as a single joint expert.

Consider the different needs of different readers. You may want to modify the approach in the report according to its purpose.

## Investigation of Facts

Make a proper detailed investigation of the facts. Full investigation and research are essential. You may discover facts by observation or from documents by yourself or with the help of others. Do not make any unnecessary assumptions. Note carefully the sources of your facts, you will need to include these in the report.

If you are instructed by both parties, be particularly careful about having separate contact with either party, or their lawyers, especially on the telephone or at a meeting – whenever possible tell the other party in advance of the planned contact, e.g a site visit, and make a note for your file which you should consider copying to the other party.

## Keep Fully Informed

To write an excellent report, you need to be fully informed of all relevant aspects of the case. You need to have access to all of the facts on which you are to base your expert opinion. You should ask the lawyers to provide you with the relevant documentation. You may be a better judge of what is and is not relevant to the issues upon which you are giving your expert opinion. As the case develops, check with the lawyers to make sure you have been given any additional documentation or relevant evidence. If you need to go back to the witnesses to get further details, do not be afraid to do so.

## Know Who Will Read the Report

Usually, the expert's report for use in proceedings will be read by the parties, the parties' lawyers, the other parties' experts and, most importantly, by the decision maker – the judge (and jury in Crown Court criminal trials) or magistrates. The report must be capable of being understood by all these people who are not experts in the field.

The report must be easy for the reader to understand. The judge will be a busy person who may not be at all familiar with the specialist/

technical area that you are writing about. Aim to avoid jargon and set out the facts and your opinion in an interesting and easy-to-understand way. Explain any technical terms clearly. Make the report as accessible as you can with a detailed contents page indicating where the facts of the case are set out, where the opinion can be found and where your conclusion is.

## What Does the Reader Need to Know?

You cannot write a report for use in legal proceedings in the same way that you write a document to be read by another professional in your field. A report which is to be used in legal proceedings must be set out so that the person reading it can find what they need for the case. A full discussion of the facts and your analysis of them, with a clear conclusion set out, are essential.

## Find Out What You Will Be Paid and How Much Time You Will Have to Write the Report

The amount of time you have to write the report and the amount you will be paid are the key parameters. These need to be made clear at the time you receive your instructions. Are you required to provide a Rolls Royce service or a Reliant Robin? If you need more time than you are offered, find out if this is possible. Time limits set by the court are vital. If the solicitor misses a court set time limit, the case may be dismissed or your late report will not be allowed into evidence. Be clear when your report is needed.

## Fact and Opinion

An expert witness is a witness who gives evidence of facts and his or her opinion on those facts.

There are different sorts of facts: facts observed by the expert – what was said and written, measurements, readings, recordings, results of experiments or inspections. There are also facts reported to the expert by a patient or client or another member of the experts' team. An expert witness gives an opinion about the facts. The expert is entitled to give an opinion because of his/her *qualifications* and/or *experience* in a particular field.

It is essential to have a foundation of facts on which to base an opinion. A reasoned and considered opinion must be based on facts. An opinion which is not supported by factual evidence will be given little weight or credit by the decision maker in court. An example of a fact is that a concrete foundation to a building was one metre thick. An opinion given on this fact by a surveyor is that this was adequate for the building in question. The opinion part in a report is essential for setting out all the possible arguments on a set of facts and illustrating the strengths and weaknesses of those arguments.

## Independence of the Expert

An expert witness must give an independent view of the case. An excellent report does not mean one that paints a rosy picture of one client's case. An excellent report is one that clearly sets out the strengths and weaknesses of the case in issue so that the parties know where they stand. As an expert, you are not a hired gun or an advocate. You are a witness whose duty is to help the court.

The Protocol on the Instruction of Experts to give Evidence in Civil Claims states:

"Experts should provide opinions which are independent, regardless of the pressures of litigation. In this context, a useful test of "independence" is that the expert would express the same opinion if given the same instructions by an opposing party. Experts should not take it upon themselves to promote the point of view of the party instructing them or engage in the role of advocates."

This requirement was developed from the remarks of Mr Justice Cresswell in the case of *National Justice Compania Naviera SA v Prudential Assurance Co Ltd (the Ikarian Reefer)* [1993] 2 Lloyd's Rep 38, in which he set out specific guidelines for experts' reports as follows:

- Independent product.

- Objective and unbiased opinion.

- Include all the relevant facts.

- Admit limits of expertise.

- Qualifications to the report must be stated.

- Changes of opinion must be communicated.

- Relevant materials must be with the report.

These guidelines were adopted by Lord Woolf in the drafting of CPR Part 35 and the Practice Direction.

Clearly, it is permissible to seek to persuade the readers of your report that there are more strengths than weaknesses in your opinion, but a report which sets out what the weaknesses are and deals with them effectively is more credible than one which ignores them. The expert should aim to appear honest and flexible in his/her approach.

## THE CONTENT OF AN EXCELLENT REPORT

In Appendix 2 on page 153 is a model report as recommended by Bond Solon. This model is only a suggestion and how you create your own personal format will depend on your specialist field. A report is not a letter and should not be set out in the style of a letter.

If your report is for use in civil court proceedings, the Civil Procedure Rules, Part 35 (the Practice Direction) and the Protocol requirements (see Appendix 4) should be followed meticulously. If your report is for use in criminal proceedings, the Criminal Procedure Rules Part 33, and the CPS Disclosure Manual Annex K, must be followed.

Note in particular the need to:

- Address the report to the court, e.g. by a covering page with the formal title of the action.

- Include a declaration that the expert has complied with his/her duty to the court.

- Include a statement of truth, i.e. that the facts and opinions in the report are correct to the best of the expert's knowledge.

The following is a suggested general format and can be modified to suit your own purposes and the court rules or directions in a particular case.

## A. Front page

The front page should state the status of the report and to whom it is addressed: note that the Civil Procedure Rules require reports for use in evidence to be addressed to the court.

*Name*

The expert's full name.

*Date*

The report must be dated the day you sign it and send it to the recipients. It should not be dated the day you interviewed the patient or went to the scene; these dates will appear in the report itself. The date indicates that your knowledge is up-to-date. If anything new comes up, then this can be added.

### Field

Set out your specialist field, e.g. plastic surgeon, surveyor, etc.

### Party

You must state whether you are giving evidence for the defendant or the claimant or are instructed by both (in civil cases), or the defendant or the prosecution (in criminal cases).

### Solicitors

Give the name of the party(ies) you appear to give evidence for, such as Mrs J Bloggs, and the name of the solicitors by whom you are instructed.

### Summary of case

Briefly set out the subject matter. For example "this is a breach of contract case involving the supply of heating equipment."

### Personal details

You also need to state your own personal details – your name, your professional address, telephone number, fax number and e-mail address if you have one.

### References

If the case has already been started by the claimant, then ask the solicitors for the court reference number and the title of the action. The names of the parties are also set out, e.g. Smith v Jones in civil cases or R v Brown in criminal cases. The "R" stands for Regina, the Crown.

## B. Headers on each page

Set out at the top of each page your name, your specialist field and the name of the party(ies) instructing you, including whether they are the claimant or defendant.

This means that if any pages are lost or pulled out it is easy to identify them.

## C. Contents page

This is essential to give quick access to the report.

## D. The main part of the report

### 1. Introduction

*1.01 The writer's full name and specialist field*

Do not give too much detail here. The full details of the expert's qualifications and experience should be set out in an appendix to the report.

It is essential that these full details do go in as they will often be scrutinised by the opposing party or by the court. It is your experience and qualifications that allow you to give opinion evidence. Do not be over modest! Remember, practical experience is just as important as research or publications.

If you are referring to publications, attach them or extracts to the report. Does your opinion in the present case reflect your opinion in the publication? If not, be prepared to explain why your view is different now.

*1.02 Summary of case*

Give a *short* synopsis of the facts and say on what you have been asked to give an opinion. For example:

The claimant was a cyclist knocked off his bicycle by an overtaking car. The claimant sustained injuries to his right leg and right arm. I have been asked to provide a medical opinion on the extent of these injuries.

### 1.03 Summary of conclusions

Do not write a suspense novel. Tell the reader what your conclusion is going to be. This enables the reader to focus on your arguments as he or she reads the report. Your opinion (see paragraph 4 below) is wide ranging, covering the possibilities and examining strengths and weaknesses in the parties' cases. Your conclusion sets out in brief what you concluded, having taken all these factors into account.

### 1.04 The parties involved

List the people and organisations you will refer to in your report, with a short description of each. This helps the reader to understand the case.

### 1.05 Technical terms and explanations

Explain that you will put any technical terms in **bold type** and explain them when first used, and also put these terms in a glossary in an appendix to the report. The glossary should be in alphabetical order.

### 2. The issues to be addressed

This is not the place to set out your opinion. It is the place to set out clearly the summary of your instructions and what the issues are.

The Civil Procedure Rules require, in civil cases, that you summarise the material instructions "both written and oral" on which the report is based. The instructing solicitor(s) may assist by setting these out for you in a letter or letters, especially if you were retained before proceedings started as an adviser and the instructions for the litigation have "evolved over time" and/or may cover issues which are no longer being pursued in the claim. If in doubt about what form part of your instructions, check first with the solicitors. One solution is to annex to the report the key solicitors' letters, especially if you are acting as a single expert and the instructions from the parties are quite different.

In any event, remember that the court may have the power, in exceptional circumstances, to order the disclosure to the court, and the other party, of the actual solicitor/expert correspondence, so do not be tempted or persuaded to be "economical with the truth".

Be clear on whether you are advising on liability and causation (that is who/why the incident was caused and the link between that and the claimants' losses), or whether you are advising on quantum (that is the extent of the injury or damage, to help the court decide how much money to award the injured party). You may be providing figures, e.g. accountants may be asked to calculate loss of earnings, loss of pension, etc.

### 3. The investigation of the facts

This paragraph is for setting out facts alone. Do not mix up facts and opinion. This is one of the most common mistakes that expert witnesses make.

It is essential to build up a detailed foundation of facts upon which you will later base your opinion. You should identify separately:

(i) Facts you observed yourself, e.g. from investigations or experiments.

(ii) Facts you were told by a patient or by others working on your behalf.

(iii) Facts which you assumed or were asked to assume. Be careful of such assumptions. As far as possible try to establish a fact rather than assume it.

(iv) Opinions of others which you considered in forming your opinion.

Remember that this is your report and you must be able to justify the foundation of fact upon which you base your opinion.

### 3.01 Assumed facts

If you have been told in your instructions to assume certain facts, set these out here. If the facts are open to interpretation, set out your interpretation of the facts and why you have taken this approach.

### 3.02 Documents

Identify key documents. In the appendix you will have copies of key documents and a list of all the documents you considered in coming to your expert opinion. You may have photocopies of pages from text books.

### 3.03 Interviews and examinations

Give details of interviews, examinations and inspections. Keep records of the dates and times, and how long they took. Also say who else (if anyone) was present.

### 3.04 Research

Give details of research you carried out or research papers you referred to. Copies of these papers, or extracts from them, should appear in the appendix.

### 3.05 Tests and experiments

Did you do them? If so, what did you do and what were the results? If someone else did them, say so and say what their qualifications and experience are. Say how you checked the results and how the system in your laboratory works.

### 4. The opinion

You should set out each of the issues, such as "did the defendant cause the claimant injury?", then link these issues with the facts and give your reasoned argument and your opinion on these facts. Do not set out all the facts in detail again in this section.

If there is a range of professional opinion on an issue, set this out and explain where your opinion lies within the spectrum, with reasons: the Civil Procedure Rules and the Criminal Procedure Rules expressly require this.

The opinion is the most important part of your report. You should aim to set out why you think your opinion is right. Highlight the strengths of your argument. If you have seen the other expert's report, set out their opinions or range of opinions briefly and comment upon them. If you have not seen the other party's expert's report, try to anticipate their opinions. Explain the weaknesses in these opinions.

Address inherent weaknesses in each party's case. Where there are two experts separately instructed, the other expert will spot the weaknesses in "your" party's case so it is best to acknowledge them and deal with them. It makes your report more credible and independent. Try to look at all the possible arguments that might be put forward and deal with these in your report, e.g. what are all the possible causes of lung cancer? In civil cases the court rules require you to do this. You are being paid to think. Think what the expert called for the other party will say. Try to address these issues in your report and comment on them.

Above all, your intention should be to ensure the reader, especially the judge, understands the reasoning behind your opinion and the conclusion of your report.

Do not try to do the judge's job. The judge decides if someone has been negligent. You are not in a position to say that someone is negligent. You are there to say whether, in your opinion, for example the doctor or the surveyor fell below the standard of a reasonable expert in the field placed in the same situation.

At the end of your opinions, put your conclusion again. The judge needs a conclusion.

## E. Statement of Compliance, Statement of Truth and Signature

In civil claims, each report must include a declaration that the expert understands and has complied with their duty to the court and a statement of truth – that the facts and opinions stated in the report are true. Check and use the exact wording in the rules and practice directions. In criminal cases the report must contain a statement of compliance (CrPR 33.3(l)(i)) and a declaration. See Appendix 6. The case of *Toth v Jarman* (see above) also suggests that a statement of conflicts should be included.

Sign and date your report the day you send it out. This dates your knowledge at that time. If anything changes, you may need to update your report.

## F. Appendices

1. *Experience and qualifications.* Set these out in date order. Explain what your qualifications entail. State any promotions or positions of responsibility you have had. Remember that a judge or jury may not be familiar with the hierarchy in your profession, and explain it.

2. *List of documents examined, copies of key documents.*

3. *List of published material referred to and copies of extracts.*

4. *Photographs, maps, diagrams, models, etc.* These can really help the judge/jury understand technical areas of the case. It is not usually possible to turn up with these things at the trial. Copies must be provided to the other party on disclosure. All such documents must be clearly labelled. It is useful to have cross-references in the report to the documents or visual aids.

5. *Chronology of events.*

6. *Glossary of technical terms* (set this out in alphabetical order).

## THE FORM OF AN EXCELLENT REPORT

The form, or way a report looks, is very important. It may be an essential tool to aid settlement of the case or the decision at a trial. It must be accessible, that is easy for people to find their way around. It should enable them to understand what the case is about. It should clearly set out your opinion. Poorly presented and organised documents can slow down the progress of the trial. It will be irritating for the judge if he or she cannot find their way around the report and it will be embarrassing for you if you cannot find your way around your report and direct the court to important areas of it.

The presentation of the report can affect the weight given to its contents.

Aim to present complex ideas in a way that can be understood. State the obvious and use simple, clear language. Your report is an essential tool for the judge to use in reaching his/her decision.

The following are tips on how to present your report:

1. Use **clear headings** – clearly define where you have set out a summary of the facts, your opinion and your conclusion.

2. Have a **contents page**, with reference to page numbers and/or paragraph numbers.

3. Use **page numbers** and **paragraph numbers**. Make sure cross-references to the appendices are included and are accurate.

4. Have **headers** on each page.

5. Have a **front page** which is visible through a transparent cover. This sets out vital details about the case.

6. Make sure there is a **clear conclusion**, which is your conclusion. Do not let anyone lean on you into writing a conclusion with which

you do not agree. You will come unstuck under cross-examination if you did not come to that conclusion on the facts. You must be independent.

7. Consider including a **chronology** to help the judge. A useful chronology might be a list of all the dates that you examined a patient or visited a site.

8. Include a **synopsis – a summary of the facts**. This will help the judge to focus on the relevant facts and understand what the case is about.

9. Make sure your report is **signed** by you personally and contains any necessary declarations and statements of truth and is **dated** the day you send it out.

10. Include an alphabetical **glossary** of technical terms that are used in the appendices. It may be helpful to use bold script followed by a definition for technical terms in the body of the report.

11. Include **graphics**, photographs, diagrams or models that will help the judge understand the case.

12. Separate **fact** from **opinion**.

13. Do not allow anyone to rewrite your report for you. They can change the emphasis of your opinion. Also it is easy for the judge to spot differences in style.

14. Write in the first person – "I"; it is your report, you sign it. Even if a team of people within a company have worked on a report, one person will have to be the expert witness (or if there are several areas of expertise, one person from each area of expertise). A report should not be signed in the company's name.

    For example, at a planning enquiry, the director of a company may have to write a final report in which he has to give his opinion on why an electricity pylon should be put in a particular place. He will include in his report the facts and opinions given to him by a range of other experts, such as an environmental expert, a construction engineer, a geologist and a civil engineer. Although the report includes facts and opinions from a number of people, it is not a joint report, signed by several people. However, each of these individuals may be asked to write separate reports and each may be called to give evidence in their own field of expertise.

15. Set out your **qualifications** and **experience** in full in the appendices. Make sure what you set out is relevant to the case in which you are giving your expert opinion. Your qualifications should be briefly explained – do not just set out a string of letters. Your experience should outline the number of years' experience you have in a particular field and the level of that experience. If you refer to positions of responsibility, explain them clearly. Mention any publications or research you have undertaken. Concentrate on your most recent and relevant experience.

16. Use A4 good quality **paper** which is hole punched and place two-inch **margins** around the paper to leave room for the reader to make notes. Use double spacing (or at least 1.5 line spacing) between the lines. It makes it easier to read.

17. **Binding**. A slide binder keeps the pages together between two plastic covers, one for the front and one for the back. Avoid comb binders as these make it difficult to photocopy the report.

18. **Printing**. Use a laser printer if possible.

19. Check the **accuracy** of the report very carefully. Mistakes, typing errors or wrong dates look bad. In cross-examination, the lawyers or the court may seek to embarrass you by picking up mistakes.

20. Make sure your final report is a **stand-alone report**. The judge should have everything he or she needs to make a decision on the technical issues in your remit in one report.

If you have written a number of disclosed reports over the life of the case, or supplementary reports, then you should rationalise them into your final report. Only very minor, last minute points are acceptable in a supplementary report form. The same applies to written questions from the parties and your answers.

For example, if you write a report on injuries to a patient after your first examination and then you examine the patient 6 or 12 months later, your findings in these first and second examinations should be together in your final report. The judge does not want to have to read two separate opinions.

21. Finally, find out **how many copies** of your report are needed and print off that many and send them. This avoids poor quality, scruffy photocopies of your report being used.

## THE WRITING PROCESS

Treat your report as a sales opportunity to "sell" yourself as an expert witness. Other lawyers and their clients may be impressed by your report and instruct you in other cases. Most importantly, you want the judge to be impressed by your report because once (s)he has read it, (s)he understands the issues, the facts and why you have reached the opinion that you have. You want to write in order to persuade the judge to understand and preferably to accept your opinion.

Remember that it is not what you write that matters, it is what the reader understands. Try to present the report in a way that is easy to understand. It is your responsibility to communicate and to take care of the reader of the report. Remember that the judge/jury and lawyers are not experts in your field. Write in a simple, clear way which will enable them to understand what the issues are and why you have reached your opinion. It may help to explain other possible opinions but then illustrate why these are not as credible as your opinion. Aim to give a good overall picture.

Make sure you remain independent – see a distinction between yourself as an expert witness giving evidence and the parties and their lawyers. Also see a difference between yourself as a person and as the writer of the report. Stand back from your report and hear in your mind all the arguments that could be put forward against your opinion. Try to counter these arguments in the report.

Writer's block can be helped by writing what comes to you first and not bothering about the order. You should write all your report and then rewrite it. Do not try to write and edit at the same time. The final version will probably be shorter than the first. As you edit it ask if each sentence gives any further meaning; go through asking "What does this say? Does it add anything?"

Use a checklist to be sure you have included the essentials required by court rules, orders and your instructions.

## WRITTEN QUESTIONS ON REPORTS IN CIVIL CLAIMS

An innovation in the Civil Procedure Rules in civil claims is the right to ask questions in writing on an expert's report within 28 days of its receipt. The rules do not prescribe a time limit for your reply but the court may do this when giving case management directions on the conduct of the action. Nevertheless, 28 days seems a reasonable guideline given that the trial may not be many weeks away, especially in Fast Track cases.

You will need to know when your report has been disclosed so you can plan the timescale for receipt of and reply to questions, so if the lawyers forget to tell you chase them.

The rules say that only clarification type questions may be asked but it seems highly likely that parties and lawyers will try to stretch this definition, particularly in Fast Track claims or any other case when oral evidence at trial from you has been ruled out. In cases where there is a single joint expert, any ambiguity in the report should be resolved by using the procedure in CPR Part 35.6 (see *Woolley v Essex County Council* [2006] EWCA Civ 753). If you receive questions which appear to require you to do further work, or which ask for comments on issues outside your report or concern your credibility, do not assume you have to answer them. Check with your instructing solicitors in a case in which both sides have their own expert or consider using your power to apply to the court for directions if you are a single expert.

You may be asked, of course, to help frame questions for the other sides' expert arising from their report.

This step in proceedings could be a very useful one if applied proportionately. It will normally take place before any experts' meeting.

# Chapter 4

# THE EXPERT WITNESS AT MEETINGS

## SUMMARY

- The purpose of the meeting •
- Preparation for the meeting •
- At the meeting •
- After the meeting •

## PURPOSE OF THE MEETING

Prior to the introduction of the Civil Procedure Rules, it was common for cases to come to trial and for a large part of the trial to be taken up with technical arguments between the expert witnesses. This was both costly and time-consuming and was generally not beneficial to the process of dispute resolution in which the court is engaged. These arguments might even leave the judge more confused about the technical aspects of the case rather than assisting him.

To overcome this, Lord Woolf introduced the experts' meeting into the litigation process. The purpose of the meeting is for the experts to identify areas of agreement and disagreement, thus saving time at trial where the cross-examination of the expert can be confined to areas of disagreement. A second purpose is that if the experts identify what is at issue between them prior to trial, this might encourage the parties to settle the dispute.

Unfortunately, there is no data indicating how successful experts' meetings have been in bringing disputes to an earlier resolution. General indications from experts are that they welcome these meetings and that they are often helpful in clarifying what is really at issue between the experts (and often the parties).

## PREPARATION FOR THE MEETING

An experts' meeting can take place at any time before or during the proceedings. Most commonly, it takes place once the experts' reports have been served on the other parties and any supplementary reports have been prepared and exchanged. A direction will usually be made at the Case Management Conference concerning when the meeting should take place. The parties may also agree at any time that a meeting should take place between the experts.

Meetings or discussions between experts should only take place where it is proportionate and therefore in small and fast track cases, they may not take place. If they do, it is more likely that they will take place over the telephone to save costs. However, in multi track cases, the Protocol suggests that the meeting should be face-to-face. If one or more of the experts is overseas, it may be more proportionate for the meeting to take place by video conference or telephone.

The meeting should always have an agenda and the responsibility for drawing up the agenda is in the hands of the parties' solicitors. However, they should do this in consultation with the expert. Drawing up the agenda can sometimes be difficult since it should indicate the areas of agreement and summarise what is in issue. If the parties cannot agree the agenda then they can ask the court for assistance.

Once the agenda has been agreed, it should be circulated to the experts in sufficient time to allow them to prepare for the meeting. When you receive the agenda, you should know what your position is on the points which are at issue and how you will substantiate what you say by reference to your report.

You should never be instructed not to agree any issues at the meeting. If you do receive instructions like this, you should consider your position as an expert and even step down. To receive such an instruction would be to instruct an expert not to fulfil their duty to the court and is clearly contradictory to the overriding duty of the expert to the court.

The parties' lawyers should not attend the meeting unless all the parties agree, or the court orders, that they should do so. If one party's lawyer attends, the meeting should not proceed unless the other party's lawyer is also in attendance. The lawyers' role at the meeting is to answer any questions that the experts might have and to advise about the law: under no circumstances should the lawyer attempt to influence the outcome of the meeting (see *Hubbard v Lambeth, Southwark and Lewisham Health Authority* [2001] EWCA Civ 1455).

## AT THE MEETING

The meeting between the experts should be a full and frank exchange of views on the matters identified on the agenda. It is not intended that the discussions should be referred to at the trial of the matter, unless the parties agree that they should be referred to. If the experts reach any agreements during the meeting, these will not bind the parties unless the parties agree that they should. Any agreement reached in either situation should be recorded in writing. Usually the parties will agree that what is agreed at the meeting will be binding, since to do otherwise will generally require the parties to explain to the court why they have refused to agree.

An expert should be able to stand their ground at the meeting but should not be afraid to recognise the validity of the other side's arguments. At the conclusion of the meeting, a statement should be prepared which sets out the list of issues that have been agreed and the basis upon which agreement was reached, as well as a list of issues that have not been agreed and the basis of the disagreement. If issues arose which were not included in the original agenda, these should be recorded, as should any further steps which need to be taken or are recommended; this might include further discussions between experts or some further investigations that need to be carried out. It is quite usual for the precise wording of this statement to be the subject of further discussion between the experts: any exchange of correspondence on this, should be marked "without prejudice" and once agreement on the wording has been agreed this wording can be removed (see *Aird v Prime Meridian Ltd* [2006] EWCA Civ 1866).

## AFTER THE MEETING

After the meeting, if there is any aspect of what was discussed which have caused you to alter your views, you should inform the solicitors instructing you as soon as possible. You must do this promptly as it may be necessary for the solicitors to give urgent consideration to settlement or to obtain further expert evidence and to apply to court for permission to call that evidence. This will not be granted automatically since the court will want to protect against "expert shopping" but it may be permitted if there is some special reason; in particular, if the party would feel an understandable sense of grievance if permission is not granted (see *Stallwood v David and Adamson* [2006] EWHC 2600 (QB)).

## Chapter 5

# THE EXPERT IN COURT

### SUMMARY

- The expert's role
- Technical preparation
- Personal preparation
- What happens in court
- What happens in the witness box
- Giving evidence and handling cross-examination
- Recognising and dealing with lawyers' techniques
- How to direct your answers
- The qualities of good evidence giving
- Finding out the result

*In this chapter, the word "court" is used to include any formal legal forum, e.g. tribunals, arbitrations, investigations and planning enquiries, and the word "judge" to refer to the decision maker.*

## THE EXPERT'S ROLE IN COURT

The expert witness is not in court to win the case, that is the job of the advocates. Even when the expert is instructed and paid by one side, his/her role is to give independent evidence to assist the court and not be a hired gun. You should be objective and impartial. You are there to give honest, independent professional opinion. You must maintain your integrity and tell the truth, the whole truth and nothing but the truth.

Your good name is your greatest asset as an expert witness. Do not distort your opinion to "win" one case.

You can, however, when instructed by one party only work to the best of your ability for them. You can bring out the strengths in the factual evidence from which you reached your opinion, and point out the weaknesses in the arguments put forward by the other party's expert.

Your overriding duty is to assist the court in reaching its decision. You need to be able to explain the technical aspects of your opinion in a clear, confident, succinct and interesting way. You are trying to persuade the judge or jury that your opinion is the best one on a given set of facts.

## PLANNING FOR THE TRIAL

An important part of the civil justice reforms is the provision of early trial dates for the parties and lawyers to work towards. Part of the judges' case management role is to set a trial date, or "window" of a few weeks, as soon as possible after the case is allocated to a track. The lawyers should check your availability when completing the allocation questionnaire, especially for Multi Track cases when oral evidence from you is more likely to be necessary.

However, be aware that trial dates will not be set or rearranged, particularly close to the event, for your convenience. The Court of Appeal has already said that detailed reasons for an expert's non-availability for a preferred trial date must be given to the judge fixing the date and that experts with busy court practices must be prepared to plan their work around the court's needs – even NHS consultants! (*Matthews v Tarmac Brick and Tile* [1999] EWCA Civ 1574). If one expert is not available for the selected trial date, the court is likely to say "Find another expert"! Similarly, the parties cannot leave it to the last minute to decide that they wish to call expert evidence (*British Sugar Plc v Cegelec* [2004] EWCA Civ 1450).

The lawyers must tell you when the trial date has been fixed for you to diary it immediately. Chase them if they do not. They must also tell you

if any other orders have been made by the court which either require
you to do something or affect you as an expert in some way.

The other important innovation is that in larger claims the judge will
often hold a pre-trial review after the listing questionnaires have been
returned – about eight weeks before trial, partly to plan the timetable
for the actual event, particularly if it is scheduled for several days or
more. The advantage of this from your point of view is that you should
be given a more specific time to attend court and not just asked to be
there for the whole trial, unless that is strictly necessary.

It is vital, of course, for you to tell the solicitors should there be any
last minute reason whatsoever which will prevent you attending when
required.

## WHAT THE JUDGE WANTS

To fully understand your role it is useful to understand how the judge
approaches the evidence of an expert witness.

This is best summarised by Stuart Smith L.J. who described in *Loveday
v Renton* ([1990] 1 Med LR 177 at 125) how the judge will approach
the evidence of an expert witness:

"This involves an examination of the reasons given for his opinions
and the extent to which they are supported by the evidence. The
judge also has to decide what weight to attach to a witness's opinion
by examining the internal consistency and logic of his evidence. The
care with which he has considered the subject and presented his
evidence; his precision and accuracy of thought as demonstrated
by his answers; how he responds to searching and informed cross-
examination, and in particular the extent to which a witness faces up
to and accepts the logic of a proposition put in cross-examination or
is prepared to concede points that are seen to be correct; the extent
to which a witness has conceived an opinion and is reluctant to re-

examine it in the light of later evidence, or demonstrates a flexibility of mind which may involve changing or modifying opinions previously held; whether or not a witness is biased or lacks independence..."

Clearly, a well prepared report (see Chapter 3) goes a long way towards showing a logical approach, highlighting facts and opinions, and strengths and weaknesses in the various experts' opinions. However, it is important that you maintain this clear, logical, calm approach while giving evidence.

The judge has a difficult job in deciding cases (as does a jury in a criminal trial). The judge needs to trust you as someone who is believable and who can materially assist him or her in deciding the case. Judges are worried about making the wrong decision and whether their decision may be appealed. They want the expert to help them come to the right decision. An extreme example of this can be found in the case of *Kirin-Amgen Inc and Others v Hoechst Marion Roussel Ltd and Others* [2004] UKHL 46, where the Law Lords who were hearing this patent infringement case had seminars by an eminent professor to educate them in the complex DNA technology which was the subject matter of the dispute.

The judge may not know about your field and, in any event, will not know as much as you, the expert witness. If the judge or the barristers did have your knowledge, you would not be needed. You are there in the role of an educator, someone to help the non-experts understand a difficult area. It may help to think of good teachers you knew and model yourself on the way they taught difficult concepts.

You are *very important; you are a key witness*. You examined the patient or the DNA samples – the court wants to hear your evidence. The judge needs to hear you clearly and understand your evidence. The biggest compliment you can be paid by the judge is "Thank you, I understand the case now!"

### What the Judge is Thinking

Once you arrive at court do not *concern* yourself with what the judge is thinking about you. Regard the judge as being neutral. Once in court, concentrate on yourself and your evidence giving. You should only think about dress and appearance *before* you go to court (see below).

## PREPARATION FOR THE HEARING

### When Does Preparation Start?

Preparation for a trial does not start a few days or even a few weeks before the trial. Preparation for trial starts as soon as you, the expert, receive instructions to prepare a report for the court, and every telephone call, letter or note should be thought of in that context.

Even though you may be asked initially to prepare a preliminary advice or report, you should be aware that the case might end up in court.

Also be aware that every day in your job as a doctor, nurse, surveyor or DNA analyst, your findings and notes could be the subject of later court proceedings. Make sure you keep proper notes of what you have done, when and why. Record reasons for professional decisions.

### Technical Preparation

1. **It is essential that you carry out a detailed, vigorous investigation/research into the facts of the case.** You need to get as much *evidence* of *fact* as you can. When doing your investigation, have an open mind. Gather all the facts. You must build a foundation of fact upon which to base your opinion. An opinion which is not based on fact will be an opinion that can quickly be shot down in court.

   Your facts may come in many different forms. Some facts you will have observed or measured yourself, some you will have been told by a patient (for example), some you will have been told by people in your research team who carried out the investigation. You must say *where* the facts came from. Distinguish between facts you observed and facts you were told.

2. **Make sure you get *all the available information* from the instructing party or solicitors.** Some may try to shape the result of your findings by only giving you some of the information. This can be disastrous if at trial an opposing advocate puts to you in cross-examination evidence you have not seen before.

   Keep asking the lawyers if they have any more documents or witness statements, especially after disclosure. *Be proactive.*

   Do not rely on the parties or the lawyers to spot all the issues. They may have a limited knowledge of the issues within a specialist or technical field. You are the expert, you are being *instructed* to give an expert opinion.

   Ensure that you are up-to-date on all your information and/or update your report.

3. **Create a working relationship with the lawyers.** Do not be afraid to ask them if you do not understand what you are supposed to be doing. Help the lawyers to understand the technicalities of the case. This will help both your and their preparation.

   When you are being instructed by one party only encourage the lawyers, particularly the advocates, to ask you the right questions. Note that this is not the same as the lawyers training you to give particular answers! Help the lawyers to formulate questions to ask the expert(s) called by the other party (you may have been asked to do this already for the written questions to be put to the other expert). You will be able to spot the weaknesses in their evidence. Remember, often the advocates may only have the papers for a short time before trial.

It is usually necessary to meet your party's advocate before the trial. Ask your instructing solicitors to arrange a "conference with counsel". This is a meeting at which you can discuss the main issues in the case.

4. **Write your report** (see Chapter 3). Make sure it is independent. Do not change your opinion under pressure from anyone. If your opinion changes from the time you wrote the report to the time the case is to be heard in court, tell the lawyers. Be very clear in your recommendations and conclusions in your report. It will help to focus your oral evidence giving.

5. **Identify the strengths and weaknesses in the case.** Look at all the possible arguments. DO NOT LEAVE ALL THE THINKING UNTIL YOU GET TO COURT. Think of likely questions that will be put in cross-examination. Remember that the cross-examining advocate will ask critical questions designed to expose the weaknesses in your opinion. Be ready to turn away from weaknesses and play to strengths in your case.

   Remember – most cases are really won and settled out of court, not in court. This preparation is vital.

6. **Prepare any graphs, plans, photographs or visual displays that will help the judge/jury understand your evidence.** Do not leave doing this until the last moment. If you do, the court may not allow you to use it. Let the lawyers know what visual aids you will need to use in court well in advance. As you write your report, think how you will explain what you are writing about; this will help you think of visual displays that may be useful.

7. **Make sure your files and documents are in good order and correctly paginated.** This will enable you to remain in control of your evidence giving. Remember to use your report to illustrate why you have reached your opinion.

8. **Ensure you are familiar with documents. Re-read notes and, most importantly, re-read your report.** Evidence giving is not a memory test but you need to be able to find your way around your report, quickly and accurately. This will avoid you becoming flustered. It helps to be able to point out to the judge diagrams, research notes, etc. in your report. This reinforces your opinion. Do not annotate your report even though you may want to highlight parts. It looks strange if you annotate it and the judge or lawyers may ask you to refer to the court copy of the report not the one you take into the box.

9. **Keep an indexed record of all your published work.** You may be asked questions about this in court. Be prepared to talk about your qualifications and experience, they give you credit as an expert – they outline the area of your expertise. Think of phrases that describe your qualifications and experience concisely and powerfully.

10. **Prepare a chronology, if necessary.** A list of times and dates can be useful if there are many details to go through.

### Personal Preparation

1. **Agree your fees as soon as possible,** including fees for cancelled appearances.

2. **Make a list of all the things you need to take with you to court.** For example, your report, documents, visual aids, your glasses or any medication.

3. If you have not given evidence before, **visit a court** and sit in on a court hearing – preferably the court where you will be giving evidence – so you can see the layout and procedure. Ask the lawyers to give you as many tips as they can about who will be in court, what a particular barrister is like, etc.

4. **Find out when the trial is and how long it is going to last**
   and for how long you might be expected to give evidence.
   Lawyers will know, especially in longer civil cases, some time
   before the trial what dates the trial is likely to be. This is because
   they will be given a fixed date for it or will at least know the "trial
   window".

5. **Find out *where* the court is and *how* you will get there,** e.g.
   by train, bus or car. Is there parking available, etc? Find out *when*
   you need to be there and where to go when you get there. Some
   courts (e.g. the High Court in the Strand) are like rabbit warrens.
   It is best to *arrange to meet* the instructing solicitors at a particular
   place and time so they can take you to the relevant courtroom.
   Ask where you can get food or drinks and where the lavatories
   are.

6. **Clear your diary** and sort out your domestic arrangements. Make
   sure you allow for more time in court than is initially suggested.
   Sometimes trials last longer than originally planned, particularly if
   there are adjournments.

7. **Plan what you are going to wear!** Make sure that you have
   some changes of clothes if you are going to be giving evidence
   for several days. Wear smart, professional clothes – dark suits or
   dresses, white or pale plain shirts or blouses. The most important
   thing is to feel comfortable and professional. Imagine you are
   dressing for an important job interview. You do not want to look out
   of place in the courtroom.

8. **Prepare your introduction.** It is a good idea to prepare your
   introduction to the court – that is your name, professional address,
   qualifications and experience – and rehearse this and get a
   colleague to comment on how you are coming across.

9. Try some **techniques for relaxation and confidence**. For example, visualise yourself in court giving evidence with confidence and power.

10. **Be aware of the date of the trial.** Tell the lawyers well in advance dates that are difficult for you and why, e.g. because you are on holiday or giving evidence in another trial. Keep the lawyers updated on a three-monthly basis on difficult dates. It may be possible to arrange the trial around these dates. As soon as you receive the letter telling you the date of the trial, book the time in your diary. If for some reason it is impossible for you to go on that date, tell the solicitor immediately. Notify your employer and any other people who have been helping you in the case preparation, of the trial date.

11. **Consider attending a training course on giving evidence.** This will help your confidence enormously, whether you have given evidence before or not.

**Preparation on the Day Before Going to Court**

Review your notes again and ensure that all your information is clear in your mind. Prepare everything you need for your appearance to avoid rushing around on the day itself. Phone the solicitor to confirm the meeting time and check your diary is clear and that all your colleagues are covering your work, etc. Finally, have a relaxing evening and an early night!

**On the Day You Go to Court**

Arrive at court early and meet the lawyers. Find out where the waiting room is and any other facilities, such as the lavatories and refreshment area. Tell the solicitor where you will be.

As an expert witness, you will usually be allowed to sit in court to watch. A witness of fact has to wait outside the court. Your place is usually behind the lawyers. When instructed by one party only you can help prompt the lawyers by making notes of questions to ask the other party's expert witness. Write any questions on a clean sheet of paper, date and time it and pass it forward. The advocate can look at it when ready so you do not interrupt the flow of his or her advocacy.

Check with the solicitor who you can and cannot speak to. Generally, you should not talk to the other witnesses or parties in the case. While you are giving evidence under oath, you must not discuss your evidence with anyone whether they are involved in the case or not; this includes lawyers or counsel.

## WHAT HAPPENS IN COURT

### Layout of the Courtroom

The judge will be at one end of the room, sitting behind a bench on a raised platform. (In criminal trials in the Crown Court, there will be a jury as well as the judge; the jury sits in a separate area. In Magistrates' Courts there will be three lay magistrates, i.e. non-lawyers or a stipendiary magistrate sitting alone, and a legally qualified clerk. In tribunals there will be a panel of usually three people. Usually one is legally qualified.)

Directly in front of the judge will sit the clerks and officials. The witness box will be at the side of the room, and is usually raised and square. The lawyers sit behind tables facing the bench (i.e. the judge). At the front will be the advocates, behind them the solicitors and expert witnesses. Members of the public may be sitting in the public gallery and there may be press present in court.

Before your first court appearance, you should visit a courtroom to see how things work and the way everything is positioned.

## The Order of the Proceedings

*(See Chapter 1 for detail on procedure and personnel in criminal and civil trials.)*

1. The advocates will make an opening speech explaining their version of events.

2. The claimant presents his/her case (through the lawyers). The claimant's witnesses will be called to the witness box. They may be questioned by the claimant's lawyers or the witness statements may be taken "as read" and they are then cross-examined by the defence.

3. The defence then present their case, calling their witnesses (for examination) and cross-examination.

4. The lawyers each summarise the evidence they have presented (closing speech).

5. The judge gives his or her decision, possibly after a short break. In more complicated cases, the judgment may be "reserved" and delivered later, sometimes in writing.

6. In civil trials of less than one day, the judge will also usually decide on the detailed legal costs at the end of the trial. In longer cases, the judge will only decide in principle who should pay the costs and the detail will be settled later by agreement or assessment (previously known as taxation).

## WHAT HAPPENS IN THE WITNESS BOX?

As a general rule, witnesses of fact cannot take notes or statements into the witness box. Expert witnesses are allowed to look at their reports and other documents but if you need to refer to notes during your evidence giving, the lawyer will have to ask permission from the judge. All the documents to be used at the trial by any witnesses will be contained in the "court bundle". If you need to see any of these documents, you will be given the bundle.

When it is time to give your evidence, you will be called by one of the court officers. You may already be sitting in court. You should stand up in the witness box, although you may sit down with the permission of the judge, after you have taken the Oath/Affirmation.

You will be asked to take the *Oath* or *Affirmation*.

## The Oath and Affirmation

The Oath is a promise on the Bible or other holy book to tell the truth. The affirmation is simply a promise to tell the truth, not based on a holy book. Decide before you go to court whether you wish to swear or affirm. It is *entirely* up to you which you choose to do – they carry equal weight. You will be asked to read the words from a card or paper in front of you and, if swearing the oath, to hold the holy book in your uplifted right hand. Take your time to read slowly, clearly and audibly, facing the judge. Stand still with your feet slightly apart and your legs straight. Do not look up while reading from the card.

*The Oath* – "I swear by Almighty God that the evidence I shall give shall be the truth, the whole truth and nothing but the truth" (for the Bible; different wording is used for other holy books).

*The Affirmation* – "I do solemnly, sincerely and truly declare and affirm that the evidence I shall give shall be the truth, the whole truth and nothing but the truth."

## Examination in Chief

The purpose of any examination in chief is to enable the judge to hear the witness's oral evidence in his/her own words. But, increasingly, the court dispenses with this, especially in civil trials and particularly if the judge has had the time/opportunity to read the papers in advance. If there is an examination in chief, it will start with you giving your name and professional address; sometimes the advocate will ask you to state your name and address, sometimes they will just ask you to confirm it. You will be asked "Is this your report?"

You may also be asked to talk about your qualifications and experience. They must be accurate. Do not be over modest – this is your opportunity to outline your expertise. Remember that you are being paid for your expertise so this is no time to hide it. Concentrate on the area of your expertise that is relevant to the case; it is useful to outline your experience in chronological order. For example, say how long you have been an accountant, say how long you have been a partner, and say what experience you have in the particular area the trial is concerned with. You may wish to refer the judge to your detailed curriculum vitae, which is an appendix to your report.

When giving your evidence, make sure you stay within your field of expertise. It is all too easy to comment on matters just outside the circle of your expertise but it is dangerous and not the reason you are in court.

In criminal trials, you will be asked a lot of questions to bring out the evidence in your report. In civil cases, the judge may have read your report and will simply ask you to confirm that it is accurate, up-to-date and that you still agree with it.

## Cross-Examination

The purpose of the cross-examination is for your evidence to be tested. When you are instructed by one party, the other party's advocate may try to show that your information and opinion are inaccurate or unreliable or may try to elicit evidence that is beneficial to their case. If you are acting as a single joint expert, you may be cross-examined by both party's advocates. Cross-examination is a hostile process, in keeping with an adversarial system, and you should expect critical questions and, in particular, attacks on your credibility as an expert and on your expert opinion. Remember that it is the duty of the cross-examining advocate to test your evidence and this can feel quite painful – or you may enjoy it as an intellectual challenge.

### Re-Examination

This does not always take place. If it does, it is an opportunity for your party's lawyers to clarify something that may have been discussed during cross-examination.

You will then be told that you can leave the witness box and, if you are a witness of fact, whether you are released from court and free to go home. *It is possible that you may be recalled after your evidence has been given.*

When experts are instructed by both parties, it is useful for the expert to sit in court before and after giving their evidence, especially when the other experts give evidence. This means that the expert can advise the advocates on the other party's expert evidence. However, you will only be asked to do this if the client or funder of the litigation can afford to pay you for your time.

### YOUR EVIDENCE AND CROSS-EXAMINATION

As an expert witness, you are in court to give evidence of your expert opinion. This is the important thing. Try to see yourself as separate from your evidence.

The job of the lawyers, often barristers, representing the other party is to test and discredit your evidence. The opposing party's lawyers do this in cross-examination.

The lawyer who cross-examines you will often seem to be attacking you personally. Do not take any of the points raised in cross-examination personally; the lawyer is just doing his or her job. There is no need for the expert to get cross, angry or defensive. You should never get into an argument with the advocate.

As soon as you allow the advocate to get "under your skin", you may lose control of calm, professional evidence giving. The quality of the evidence you give will be affected if you are flustered and angry and trying to score points.

Attacking you personally is just one of the techniques that a lawyer will use to undermine your evidence. In particular, an opposing lawyer may try to undermine your credibility as an expert witness by attacking your qualifications and experience or by attacking your opinion. The lawyer will have had the weaknesses in your opinion pointed out to them by their expert. They will put these weaknesses to you. They will try to show that you have not got a reasoned basis for your opinion. Ensure that you outline the facts that support your opinion. An expert who states an opinion just because the client or lawyers suggested it will be found out!

There are various methods of testing a witness in cross-examination, but the following are common techniques:

1.  Trying to limit the expert's expertise by showing that the expert's qualifications and experience are inferior (for example "Why did you only attend X institution to study for your degree and not Oxbridge?") or do not apply to the case in question.

    The expert must be prepared to explain how and why his/her qualifications and expertise are relevant.

2.  Unfavourable comparisons with another expert. This will be done by suggesting the other expert is better qualified or more experienced, for example "Our expert has 25 years' experience in the field, you only have 10. How can you say our expert is wrong?". Don't be daunted by this, take time to explain your own experience and qualifications and the strengths of your opinion.

3. Asking the expert to explain jargon or technical terms. The expert should be prepared to explain simply and clearly any technical terms (s)he uses without waiting to be asked to explain them. If you use them, explain them straight away.

4. Criticism of the expert's investigation and research process. Methods may be attacked and any omissions or errors pointed out.

5. Suggesting that their expert's opinion is within a reasonable band of opinions and you cannot disagree that that opinion is legitimate. Agree it may be legitimate, but illustrate why your opinion should be preferred!

6. Trying to get you to agree with some of what the other expert says.

7. Attacking your opinion for not being based on a sound foundation of fact. Always illustrate which facts you took into account when reaching your opinion.

8. Hypothetical situations may be suggested to illustrate weaknesses in your opinion. Make sure you distinguish between the actual facts and the hypothetical facts when giving your answer.

9. Trying to get the expert to become extreme or unreasonable in their view to show bias. Do not exaggerate; do not say you are absolutely 100% certain, for few things are this certain. Remain flexible but firm. Never say "never" or "always".

The lawyer is trained to control you, the expert witness, in cross-examination. You must remain calm and confident. *Do not* become defensive or argumentative. Play to your strengths. Avoid letting the lawyer take control.

Remember your duty in court is to help, and in some cases to educate, the judge. The judge is also neutral – talk to the judge, not to the advocate asking the questions. This will help you to remain calm and to avoid getting cross with or upset by the barrister's questions. The judge may ask questions to help understand the case.

Do not be afraid of lawyers. Realise you are both professionals in court to do a job and that your roles are different.

## Who To Talk To

You should always talk to the decision maker, who is the judge or jury in a Crown Court and the magistrate(s) in a Magistrates' Court. It is the decision maker who needs to hear your evidence. Whenever you answer a lawyer's question, turn to the judge before speaking. Use the turning technique described below to help you do this.

If your evidence in the witness box is interrupted by a lunch or overnight adjournment, do not speak to anyone about the case without authority from the court. This includes your instructing solicitor.

## What To Say

Tell the truth. If you cannot remember, say so. If you do not know the answer, say so. Explain your answers if you want to. For example, why you decided, as an accountant assessing income loss, to use a particular multiplier; why as an actuary you chose 1% not 2%.

Do not comment on things about which you have no direct knowledge, for example what you think the doctor thought. Stay within your field of knowledge and expertise. If the question goes outside this area, say so and explain why you cannot answer.

## LAWYERS' TECHNIQUES AND TYPICAL QUESTIONS

It is impossible to predict exactly what a lawyer will ask you in court. Nor is your own party's lawyer allowed to "coach" you through your evidence by practising with you beforehand.

There are two areas that need to be considered: examination in chief and cross-examination.

### In Examination in Chief

When this is allowed, the lawyer for your party asks these questions. The questions are likely to follow the order of your statement or report, and you should feel free to set the pace of your answers, giving as much relevant information as you can. This is your opportunity to put across the strengths of your expert opinion. During the examination in chief, the lawyer cannot ask you "leading questions", i.e. a question that suggests the answer. The lawyer must get you to volunteer the information in your statement or report.

In civil cases, the examination in chief can be dispensed with entirely, or can be very short, as the judge should have read your report and this reading can replace the examination in chief; you may just be asked if there are any additions.

### In Cross-Examination

Cross-examination is by the other side's lawyer. As mentioned, they are seeking to discredit your evidence and so will be keen to confuse you and try to get you to contradict yourself. They will ask questions about your weaknesses not your strengths. The lawyer's tactics will be to attack the content of your evidence or occasionally to undermine you by theatrics. The overall techniques used were described in the previous section.

Below are some further examples of lawyers' tricks and techniques.

- Asking closed questions – *"Did you see the patient walk or not? Answer the question yes or no."*

- Feigning ignorance or confusion – *"How could you listen to the doctor if you were talking to the patient?"*

- Using patronising tones and sarcasm – *"Well, of course you would say that, because he is paying your fees today."*

- Making direct attacks on the ability of an expert witness – *"What made you think you could act; you've only had 18 months' experience, why didn't you get help?... What made you think you were properly qualified to do this job?"*

- Using multiple questions – *"What time did the patient arrive, what did she say, what did the nurse do when she saw the patient?"*

- Interrupting you mid-sentence – especially if you are just about to make a good point.

- Giving looks of disbelief or using a tone of disbelief.

- Shuffling papers, passing notes or whispering to colleagues.

- Focusing on tiny, irrelevant points such as an unimportant time.

- Repeating earlier questions, in the hope you will contradict yourself.

- Mispronouncing your name – *"Well Ms Frompton/Trumpton/ Frumptin."*

- Contradicting you, especially by using your opponent's expert's opinion.

- Remaining silent. You will perhaps want to fill the gap.

- Using hypothetical questions – *"What if the concrete had been two inches thicker?"*

- Jumping around in the chronology, starting at the end of your report and working backwards.

- Using jargon and asking you to explain it.

- Picking on inaccuracies in your report, e.g. typos, dates.

- Picking on inconsistencies between what you say and what other experts say.

- Asking you to speak up or slow down.

- Getting you to agree to absolutes – *"Are you 100% certain?"*

Before the case, take time to think of likely questions or lines of "attack". Write a list in your court file. The key is how to handle these questions so that you say what you want to say. This is discussed below.

## KEEPING IN CONTROL AND HANDLING LAWYERS' TECHNIQUES

**You are the one in control.** There are two very good reasons for this. The first is that, no matter how well-prepared the lawyers are, they do not know your field or evidence as well as you do. They are not experts in your field. They were not there and thus did not see it, do it or hear it, investigate or research it. You were and did! All the information the lawyer has is, at best, "second hand".

The second reason why you are in charge of your evidence is that the judge wants to hear *your* information and opinion. The better the information you give the judge, the easier it is for him or her to make a decision.

With that control in mind, how do you deal with the techniques? Identify the strengths and weaknesses in your evidence. Think in advance what the key points of your evidence are and take *every opportunity* to get them over to the court so that the court receives a balanced view of the case.

Listen to the question – often it is designed to focus on a weakness. Think how you can present your best points in answer to the question.

**Do not be distracted by the techniques.** Treat them as opportunities. If the lawyer is repeating a question, say so – "Yes, that was the point I dealt with earlier". Or if it is a long, meandering question, help the judge by breaking it down – "Well, there are three points here" or "It actually happened in this order". Ignore sarcasm and bullying. If you are asked to answer a question "Yes" or "No" you do not have to. The lawyer is asking you to do this to push you into extreme views. Say to the judge "I can't answer the question yes or no, there are a number of factors that have to be considered...".

Do not agree to absolutes, e.g. "never" or "100%". Be careful in giving estimates in relation to time, space or distance.

Take your time. Remember you are the one in control. The judge is there to see fair play. Ask the judge if you need more time to answer the question, or if you need the question repeated. In other words, do not be afraid to take charge of your information and present it in the way that you want.

Remember that the lawyers are only doing their job in using their techniques. When you visit a court and see some cross-examination in action, separate the technique from the question. For example, see that there were three looks of disbelief, two multiple questions, a long pause and so forth.

## HOW TO DIRECT YOUR ANSWERS

Remember the only person to speak to in court is the judge or magistrates (and jury in criminal cases in the Crown Court). They make the decision. Do not try to persuade the questioning lawyer, or even speak to him/her. A good way of remembering this is as follows:

- As soon as you enter the witness box, directly face the judge and point your feet at him/her. If there is a jury, include both judge and jury.

- Do not move your feet. Now twist your hips to face the lawyer.

- Look at the lawyer and listen carefully to the question. Watch out for any techniques that may be used to disconcert you.

- When the lawyer has finished his or her question, and not before, turn back to face the judge/jury. The fact that your feet are pointing that way will remind you. You have a few moments in the turning to prepare your answer. In any event, you should never hurry your answer.

- When you are directly facing the judge/jury, give your answer. You can see if the judge is with you or if you are speaking too quickly as (s)he may be writing down your answer. Do not worry if (s)he is not looking at you if (s)he is writing.

- When you have finished your answer, turn back to the lawyer slowly. This signals you are ready for the next question. If the lawyer tries to interrupt you, continue facing the judge/jury and continue with your answer.

Although this may sound unnatural, it is very easy with practice and will give you a lot of control in the speed of the questions. The judge/jury can also hear better and you will not be tempted to get into a conversation with the lawyer.

Be sure to use this technique in the witness box. It is straightforward and extremely effective in allowing you to focus on the judge/jury and ignore the lawyer when giving your answer.

## HOW TO KEEP CALM

There are various techniques you can use and may already know about. The most obvious and perhaps most important is to look after yourself, especially in the days preceding the trial.

Another tip is to use visualisation. This is a technique many successful people use, particularly sportsmen and women and business people. It involves sitting somewhere quiet where you will not be disturbed. Close your eyes, take some deep breaths and, in your mind, imagine being the way you want to be, fulfilling the criteria you have written on your list of how you want to come across. Imagine yourself remaining this way through the cross-examination, whether it is slow, quick, aggressive, calm or straightforward. You can practise this as many times as you like. When you get into the witness box for real, you will have already rehearsed your evidence and you will feel more confident because it is not completely unfamiliar to your brain. If you have not tried this kind of technique before, do try it. It is very powerful.

Use the support you have around you – friends, family or colleagues. It is a cliché, but sharing a problem or fear can often get things into perspective. Attend a confidence-building training course in courtroom skills. Remember also that even the most experienced witnesses can be nervous before going to court. Some barristers are even physically ill! You are only human.

## THE QUALITIES OF GOOD EVIDENCE GIVING

Your evidence consists of two parts: the content, which is largely set out in your report, and the presentation. Use your report to help you and the judge when you are in court.

The essence of good evidence giving is simple, clear communication. Be helpful, truthful and independent. Be a reliable source of information. The way in which you give your evidence affects the weight of credibility attached to it. Imagine that, if your evidence is clear, succinct, convincing and truthful, it will weigh down heavily on the scales of justice to help tip the balance in the favour of the party who has instructed you. If, however, your evidence is confusing, and you are nervous, aggressive, pompous, rambling and inflexible, it will be given little or no weight.

Research suggests that juries, in particular, are influenced by the *way* evidence is given rather than the evidence itself. You need to get both the evidence and the presentation right to be as effective as possible.

## About You

Aim to be friendly, warm and helpful. Do not see being an expert witness as an opportunity to be pompous and egotistical.

Listen carefully to a question and look at the questioner. Do not answer until the advocate has finished the question and you are sure you understand it. Stand up straight with your weight balanced evenly on both feet. Do not hop from foot to foot or jig around as this distracts from your evidence giving. It also makes you appear nervous. Decide where you are going to put your hands. Do not put them in your pockets. It is often best to rest them lightly on the top of the witness box. Do not grip the edge of the witness box.

Try to appear relaxed. Maintain friendly open eye contact with the judge/jury. Though you may be able to sit down, it is customary to stand until invited to sit.

Make sure you do justice to yourself. Explain your qualifications and experience with pride. Highlight those areas of your qualifications and experience that really help with the case before the court.

## Your Voice: Speed of Evidence

The voice is an important tool in evidence giving. Smiling before you go into court helps to relax the muscles in the face. This gives you more control over your voice. Holding your breath is a natural reaction to stress but it will make your voice quiver. Breathe. It will calm you down and slow you down. You must control the *speed* of your evidence giving. A good tip is to watch the judge's pen (or other presiding officer's) as they may take notes as you speak.

Make your voice interesting by altering the pitch and volume. You can use your voice to emphasise important points. Speak rather than nodding or shrugging. Avoid reading documents at the same time as speaking. If necessary, ask for a few minutes to be allowed to read the document or report.

### How to Present Evidence

Use simple, short sentences. Repetition will help ensure your key points are heard. Do not use technical language or convoluted sentences. Imagine yourself as a teacher; state the obvious and explain technical areas.

Make sure you are consistent and logical in your thought process. Consider carefully matters put to you in questions. Concede some points; for example, if asked "Would it have been better to look at 100 samples rather than 10", agree it would. But say you are confident that, with 10, you have the right answer. Be ready to be flexible but do not be bullied into changing your opinion.

If you say something that is incorrect, take the earliest opportunity to correct it.

Refer to your report as much as you can. This will encourage the judge to annotate his/her copy and refer to it when preparing his/her judgment.

### The Content of the Evidence

An expert witness gives evidence of both fact and opinion. As seen in Chapter 1, facts come from many sources. It is critical that you should distinguish between facts and opinion when giving oral evidence, in the same way as you distinguish between facts and opinion in your report.

You need to refer back to your foundation of fact before you give your opinion evidence. Thus a surveyor might refer back to the depth of concrete that he measured before saying that, in his opinion, this was insufficient for a particular building.

Do not make assumptions from one set of facts that cannot be supported by another. For example, do not assume the base cracked because the building was too heavy.

It is very important that, in giving your opinion evidence, you **stay within your field of expertise**. It is very easy to be pulled outside the circle of your expertise and to attempt to answer questions. Sooner or later you will be caught out.

Examples are: the general practitioner who attempts to answer questions on psychology or open heart surgery; the accountant who tries to answer questions on the world economy; the nurse who tries to give evidence on the biological/chemical make-up of the brain.

Finally, you must make sure that you bring out the *strengths* of your opinion under cross-examination. Expert witnesses frequently complain that during cross-examination they were asked all the wrong questions! It is up to you to make sure you bring out the strong points.

**You must take control.** Do not let the advocates control you. You must take responsibility for getting a fair picture across to the judge/jury. Be as persuasive as you can. Remember that different experts have different opinions. Do not be put off by the fact that another expert has a different opinion.

## HOW TO DEAL WITH THE OTHER EXPERTS' EVIDENCE

There will often be an expert witness called by each of the parties but increasingly in smaller civil claims the parties may agree or the court may decide there should be a single joint expert.

Where there are experts for each party, an expert witness must be prepared to *comment* on another expert witness's opinion. This can be done in the expert report, which can be updated if necessary, in a note of an experts' meeting if the parties are willing for this to form part of the evidence or in oral evidence given in court at the trial. The expert should anticipate in his/her report what the opinion of another expert might be – in reports in civil cases you should, in any event, give the range of professional opinion where you can, especially on controversial matters. The weaknesses of the other expert's opinion can then be highlighted. It is important to remember that the fact that the expert witness has a different opinion does not mean that one opinion is wrong and the other right. Be prepared to substantiate the strength of the facts or other evidence that support your expert opinion. Also try to highlight the weaknesses in the facts and evidence relied on by the other expert in reaching their opinion.

Do not completely discount the evidence of another expert. Remember that it is important to be professional at all times and that opinions do differ, but try to persuade the judge that your opinion is to be preferred, given your reasoned argument.

## FINDING OUT THE RESULT AFTER THE CASE IS OVER

If you stay until the end of the proceedings, in a criminal trial you will hear the verdict – guilty or not guilty. However, there will probably be an adjournment before sentencing; the judge will decide what sentence to give on a different day. At the end of a civil trial, the judge will usually give judgment (not a verdict) but in more complicated cases may "reserve" judgment and give it at a later date.

If you are unable to stay until the end of the trial, ask the solicitors to let you know the outcome of the trial.

Do try to get some feedback from the instructing solicitors on how your evidence came across. You may have to ask them.

## Chapter 6

# PAYMENT OF EXPERTS' FEES

### SUMMARY

- Who pays the solicitor? •
- Who is responsible for paying expert witnesses? •
- How much will you be paid? •
- When will you be paid? •
- Cancellation fees •

## INTRODUCTION

Some experts experience problems in being paid for their services. This section aims to provide some guidance on the underlying principles concerning being paid. While there is no need for the expert to understand fully the system for payment of lawyers and experts in litigation, a brief overview of this system may be of some assistance.

The way in which the legal costs of claims and litigation are paid is rapidly changing. The details of these changes are outside the scope of this book. Since 1995 personal injury (and a few other types of claims) have been allowed to be funded on a type of "no win no fee" arrangement, known as conditional fees. The solicitors, and sometimes the advocates, are paid only if they win, but then can charge an additional amount of costs known as a success fee. Since 1998 *any* type of civil money claim can be conducted on this basis. A variety of insurance products are available to support this type of funding; these usually cover payment of the claimant's expenses, including experts' fees if the case is lost, and payment of the other party's legal and other costs in those circumstances.

The Access to Justice Act 1999, which came into effect in 2000, enabled any success fee and insurance premium to be paid by a losing defendant in the litigation. The Act also withdrew legal aid funding from most types of personal injury claims, but not clinical negligence.

Also, since an important court decision in 1998, solicitors have been allowed to conduct clients' civil litigation cases on contingency arrangements, i.e. straightforward "no win no fee", provided they do not charge any more if they win than they would have done if the client was paying privately. However, the type of contingency arrangement common in the USA, where the lawyer takes a percentage of the client's damages, is not permitted here in court proceedings.

One likely impact on experts of these new funding arrangements is that in some cases solicitors will want quick initial advice from an expert on the strengths and weaknesses of the case, for a limited fee, to enable the solicitor to decide whether to take on the case on one of the "no win no fee" funding arrangements.

Also, increasing numbers of individuals and businesses have legal expenses insurance which in approved circumstances covers the legal costs of pursuing a claim and the other side's costs if the case is lost.

Large numbers of claims, of course, continue to be funded by legal aid, trade unions and by clients paying privately and many defendants are financed by liability insurance.

In civil cases, the Civil Procedure Rules give the court powers to limit the amount of expert fees which may be recoverable from the losing party. This power, even when exercised, does not affect the contract between the expert and their own client/solicitor but, where the court limits the recoverable fees in advance of an expert being instructed, the client/solicitor may seek to persuade the expert to carry out the work for the figure specified by the court.

The remainder of this chapter only covers the basic essentials on these various ways of funding litigation insofar as they have an impact on experts.

## WHO PAYS THE LEGAL COSTS?

The solicitor's bill, or "costs" as it is known in legal jargon, includes all the costs of the litigation incurred on behalf of the client who instructs them. This means the solicitor's own work, work done by barristers, experts' fees and any other expenses of the litigation. The client is contractually responsible for paying these costs regardless of the outcome of the case (although in practice in many cases the costs will be covered by insurance or by a trade union).

However, in civil cases, the loser of a case may be ordered to pay some or occasionally all of the winner's costs (except when the loser is legally aided).

If the solicitor is acting on a "no win no fee" arrangement (conditional fee or contingency fee), he/she may not be paid at all, but the solicitor/client will still be responsible for expenses, including experts' fees, and for the other side's costs. Often the solicitor/client will arrange in advance for insurance to cover these costs.

Thus, if a solicitor's client wins, their own costs may be paid in total or in part by the losing client, the Legal Services Commission or the client him/herself.

Similarly, in criminal cases a defendant found guilty may be ordered to pay prosecution costs. If found not guilty, he may be awarded costs from central funds.

To a large extent, the method by which the solicitors get paid the costs, which include the experts' fees and expenses, is irrelevant to the expert. The expert has a contract with the client or solicitors who instruct him or her. This contract is binding, irrespective of how or when the solicitors are paid.

## ASSESSMENT (OF COSTS)

In all cases funded by the Community Legal Service (previously legal aid cases), and in the case of civil cases where there are costs of the other party to be paid by a privately funded losing party, these costs will be subject to assessment if the parties cannot agree the fair amount of the costs between themselves. This means that the amount of costs incurred is looked at by the trial judge, or later by a costs judge or officer or justices' clerk, to see if it is appropriate and reasonable. Thus the lawyers' fees, counsels' fees, experts' fees and any other expenses are all looked at and the amount may be reduced or "assessed" down, to a reasonable level. The judge or official will look at the amount of time spent on any item, the hourly rate or fixed fee charged and in a civil case will also consider whether they are "proportionate" to what was in dispute.

## PRIVATELY FUNDED CIVIL CASES

### Who Is Responsible for Paying My Fees?

The contract is between you and the person, usually the solicitor, who instructs you. Solicitors will in most cases have asked their clients for funds on account to pay both your fees and your expenses. Nevertheless, it is the solicitor who is liable to pay your fees, whether or not they have been given money on account by their clients.

If you are instructed jointly by the parties, they may be jointly responsible for your fees (this is what the civil court rules provide as the starting point) or the parties might agree that one party only will pay you: the latter will clearly be easier for you.

Solicitors are responsible for paying civil court attendance fees and expenses. They will receive the money from their own client or, if their client wins, the court may order the other side to pay some of the costs.

If the solicitor is acting on a "no win no fee" type basis, this does not change the contractual obligation to pay your fees, even if the client/ solicitor loses the case. You should not agree to work on a contingency basis yourself in any type of court proceedings, even if asked to do so, as this could seriously undermine your perceived "independence and credibilty". It is specifically prohibited to act on this basis in the Protocol.

It is essential to agree the terms of your contractual agreement with the person responsible for your payment before you undertake any work. The key terms are **how much** you are to be paid and **when** you will be paid.

## How Much Will I Be Paid?

It is sensible to have a written contractual agreement which sets out how much you will charge per hour, or per report. Your hourly rate will depend on the field of your expertise and the "market rate" for similar experts.

Keep a record of the date and the time you spend on any tasks. Also keep a record of any expenses you incur, e.g. travelling, photocopying, etc. A day-to-day record should be kept – see example overleaf.

It is best for you to have a contractual agreement that sets out that, irrespective of the outcome of any assessment, the instructing solicitors must pay your fees in full. However, you may find some solicitors reluctant to enter into such an agreement and they may ask you to accept payment according to the outcome of an assessment.

Where your fees will be subject to assessment, it is crucial that you have records of the work you have undertaken so that the instructing solicitors can justify to the costs judge or officer the amount of your fees.

## Example of Time Record

| File | Date | Time Spent | Task | Hourly Rate | Total |
|------|------|-----------|------|-------------|-------|
| Jones | 11th Sept 06 | 2 hrs | Reading papers | £90 | £180 |
| Jones | 12th Sept 06 | 1 hr | Research | £100 | £100 |
| Jones | 18th Sept 06 | 1.5 hrs | Examining patient | £100 | £150 |
| Jones | 29th Sept 06 | 3 hrs | Meeting with counsel | £100 | £300 |
| Jones | 3rd Oct 06 | 6 hrs | Writing report | £100 | £600 |
| Jones | 2nd Feb 07 | 1 hr | Travelling and waiting | £60 | £60 |
| Jones | 2nd Feb 07 | 2 hrs | In court | £100 | £200 |
| Expenses | | | | | |

## When Will I Receive My Fees and Expenses?

Have a term in your contract for services which states when payment is due – 14 days or 28 days after the date of the invoice. You are entitled to ask for expenses and fees on account, i.e. before they are incurred. However, it is common practice to send in an invoice for your fees and expenses once you have incurred them. You can add interest for late payment.

You should consider carefully whether to include in your contractual agreement expenses/fees on account and interim payments. Interim payments are payments for fees and expenses as you proceed so that, at each stage of your work, you can ask for a payment on submission of an invoice. It may be possible to agree payment of expenses before they are incurred. Many experts send an invoice when they submit their report to the solicitors. Some send the invoice before the report and will only send the report after they have been paid but this is not popular with solicitors!

There is no need for you to wait until the litigation is over before submitting your invoice, if you have agreed that you will be paid earlier. However, you may be asked sometimes to wait for payment until the end of the case, especially when the solicitors will not be paid until then or at all, as in "no win no fee" arrangements. Whether you agree is up to you but, if you do this, it should not affect your independence or credibility.

## LEGALLY AIDED CIVIL CASES

### Who Is Responsible for Paying My Fees?

As in privately funded cases, the solicitor who instructs you is responsible for payment of your fees. Payment depends on the terms of the contract between the solicitor and the expert. The Legal Services Commission pays the reasonable costs of the litigation to the solicitor who is under a contractual obligation to pay the expert's fees.

### How Much Will I Be Paid?

Where the solicitor has agreed the fee, the expert will be paid in accordance with the contract and the solicitor must pay that full fee irrespective of whether this is more than the amount paid to the solicitor by the Legal Services Commission. Most experts prefer to agree fees in advance irrespective of the outcome of assessment, that is irrespective of any deductions from the fees made at a costs assessment hearing.

### Prior Authority

Many solicitors will not wish to run the risk of being liable to pay the shortfall between what the Legal Services Commission pays them and the fee agreed with the expert. In this case, they will seek prior authority from the Legal Services Commission that it is necessary to instruct an expert and that the proposed fee is reasonable. Where such authority is granted, it will state the amount of expenditure on the expert's fees which is authorised. The effect of such prior authority is that the amount of the expert's fee will be guaranteed to be paid to the solicitor (with very limited exceptions). To help gain prior authority, the expert may be asked to provide a costed programme of work. If further work is required, then the Legal Services Commission's further authority should be sought for any additional fees and expenses.

### When Will I Be Paid?

The timing of payment is also dependent on the terms of the contract between the solicitor and the expert. There is no implied term that the expert has to wait until the solicitor has been paid. The best terms are for the expert to be paid within 14/28 days of invoicing the solicitor. However, the solicitor may ask that payment should only be made within a reasonable time of the solicitor being paid on account by the Legal Services Commission. The expert must take a commercial decision as to whether the solicitor will instruct him/her if he/she insists on payment regardless of whether the solicitor is in funds from the Legal Services Commission.

It is important to note that it is *not* necessary to wait until the litigation has finished before the expert is paid. The solicitor can and should apply to the Legal Services Commission for payment on account of experts' fees and expenses incurred or about to be incurred. The expert witness should consider putting a clause in the contract with the solicitor to the effect that the solicitor will seek such payment on account from the Legal Services Commission.

## PAYMENT FOR ATTENDANCE AT COURT IN CIVIL CASES

The solicitor who instructs the expert is responsible for paying all witnesses who attend court to give evidence. Again, prior authority for the fee to be paid can be obtained from the Legal Services Commission and payment on account can be obtained.

## Cancellation Fees

There is no automatic payment of a fee where the expert's attendance at court is not required but the expert may obtain reasonably incurred expenses and/or payment for time spent in preparation. However, there is a duty to mitigate losses incurred, e.g. by rearranging appointments.

It is therefore wise to address the issue of how you will be compensated for cancellation of court appearances in your contract.

## PRIVATELY FUNDED CRIMINAL CASES

The position for payment of experts is the same as in privately funded civil cases. Fees should be agreed in advance in the contract between the solicitor and the expert. Ideally, the expert should ask the solicitor to agree to pay the full amount irrespective of the outcome of any costs assessment.

## LEGALLY AIDED CRIMINAL CASES

### Who Is Responsible for Paying My Fees?

Again, the position is similar to civil cases. The instructing solicitor is responsible for paying the expert witness for everything, with the exception in this case of attendance at court.

### How Much Will I Be Paid?

As in civil cases, the expert can agree the amount of his/her fees (apart from the attendance at court fee) with the instructing solicitor. The agreement can be for the full amount irrespective of any assessment down of the fee. However, as in civil cases, solicitors who are reluctant to face the risk of a deficit in the amount obtained after the assessment of costs by the Crown Court will apply for prior authorisation from the Criminal Defence Service of the use of an expert and the amount of expenditure.

### When Will I Be Paid?

In Crown Court cases, an interim payment/payment on account from the Crown Court can be made if the Criminal Defence Service has authorised expenditure in excess of £100 and liability to pay a disbursement of £100 or more has arisen. Thus the solicitor needs:

(i)  evidence of the prior authority; and

(ii) the expert's invoice.

There is no provision for payment on account in the Magistrates' Court.

## PAYMENT FOR ATTENDANCE AT COURT IN CRIMINAL CASES

The rule in criminal cases is different from that in civil cases. This is, firstly, because payment is from central funds and, secondly, because there is no facility for obtaining prior authority or payment on account.

In criminal cases, central funds administered by the Crown Prosecution Service pay for the witness's attendance at court. This payment can be obtained by attending the court cash office after the witness has given evidence. There should be no delay in such payment, provided that the expert's hourly rate is deemed reasonable. The amount allowed usually includes a notional one hour for preparation for the hearing.

For witnesses of fact or those classified for payment purposes as professional witnesses, payment is fixed by the Treasury. The allowances given are designed to compensate them for expenses or losses incurred in attending court to give evidence. For example, a general practitioner who has to attend court and therefore must hire in a locum can claim the expense of hiring the locum. For expert witnesses, the amount allowed will depend on their expertise and the nature and complexity of the case.

It may be disconcerting for expert witnesses to be unable to fix their fee for court attendance in criminal trials before they go to court. However, this problem cannot be avoided by refusing to attend court, since the solicitors will serve a witness summons on the expert. This obliges the expert to attend and failure to do so will amount to contempt of court and expose the witness to the risk of imprisonment.

## Cancellation Fees

Where the court hearing is cancelled because the defendant pleads guilty, the expert witness may claim reasonably incurred expenses and/or preparation expenses. However, as in civil cases, there is a duty to mitigate the loss by rearranging appointments, etc.

# APPENDICES

## Appendix 1

# PRO FORMA ENGAGEMENT LETTER
to be issued as soon as instructions or
potential instructions are received

*N.B. The Expert Witness Institute has a model terms and conditions letter on its website (www.ewi.org.uk) and also model terms and conditions of engagement. By reference to the example set out below and to these sources, you should prepare your own standard terms.*

---

```
Our ref:
Your ref:
                                    29 August 2007

Name and full address of
instructing solicitor's
firm - not an individual



Dear Sirs

Case Name

Thank you for your letter of instruction/potential
instruction dated .......

I set out below my understanding of the services
you require me to perform as an expert [accountant/
GP/surveyor/psychologist/nurse, etc.] in the above-
mentioned case.
```

Insert here a paragraph to explain what you have been engaged to do on this particular assignment; it is very important that you and the instructing

---

solicitors are both aware of the scope of your advice. This avoids later claims of negligence against you. It may fall within the following categories:

1. Preparation of a preliminary expert's report on quantum and/or liability.

   (A preliminary report is a report prepared for a solicitor to help the solicitor to decide if the solicitor's client, the claimant, has a case.)

2. Preparation of a final expert's report on quantum and/or liability.

   (This will usually take the form of an updated preliminary report, and will be on the same areas as 1. above.)

3. Preparation of a report for the defendant or the prosecution in a criminal case.

4. Attending meetings of experts to narrow the issues before trial.

5. Considering a settlement.

6. Attending conferences with counsel.

7. Attending at court for trial and/or other hearings.

Each case should be considered on its own merits and the paragraph describing the work that you are required to do should be drafted accordingly.

## Obligations of the solicitor

1) Deal promptly with every reasonable request by me for authority to obtain any information and documents deemed by me necessary to fulfil your instructions.

2) Give prompt written notification of every meeting, hearing, trial or other appointment at which my attendance will be required.

3) Not alter or permit others to alter any of the reports produced by me.

4) Notify me in writing 7 days before disclosure of my report is to be made, so final checks to update the report can be made by me before the report is disclosed.

*For civil cases:*

5) The solicitor will provide me with all documents relevant to the case, in particular:

a) the claimant's/defendant's statements;

b) the claimant's statement of claim in the High Court, or particulars of claim in the County Court and, once the case has been started, any other pleadings;

c) all claimant and defendant witness statements;

d) the reports of other experts, for both the claimant and the defendant;

e) any directions of the court as to how the case is to be conducted;

f) any other relevant documents.

*For criminal cases:*

5) The solicitor will provide me with all the documents relevant to the case, and in particular:

a) notify me of what the defendant is charged with;

b) notify me what defence if any the defendant is relying on;

c) give me the defendant's statement;

d) give me witness statements for the prosecution and defence (or summaries);

e) give me reports of the expert witnesses for both the prosecution and the defence;

f) give me any other relevant documents.

**Obligations of the expert**

As the expert, I will:

a) use reasonable skill and care in the performance of the instructions given to me;

b) act with objectivity and independence with regard to my instructions and, in the event of a conflict between my duties to your client and to the court, hold my duties to the court paramount;

c) undertake only those parts of a case in respect of which I consider I have adequate qualifications and experience;

d) promptly notify the solicitor of any matter (including a conflict of interest or lack of suitable qualifications and experience) which would disqualify me or render it undesirable for me to have continued involvement in the case;

e) use all reasonable endeavours to make myself available for all meetings, hearings, trials and other appointments of which I have received adequate written notice;

f) not without good cause discharge myself from the appointment as expert;

g) preserve confidentiality save as expressly or by necessary implication authorised to the contrary;

h) not negotiate with another party or adviser unless specifically authorised by the solicitor to do so. For avoidance of doubt this does not apply to any order of a court or tribunal.

**Intellectual property rights**

The rights of ownership in respect of all documents, photographic negatives, video recordings, models and other original work created by me shall remain vested in me unless otherwise agreed in writing.

**Fees**

My fees are based upon the degree of responsibility and skill involved and the time necessarily occupied on the work. Unless otherwise agreed, they will be charged separately for each class of work mentioned above. For example, my hourly rate for preparation of evidence is £-. My daily rate for attending a hearing is £-. I will also invoice you for any reasonable costs incurred.

Invoices for work done will be rendered at appropriate times.

**Initial review of cases**

I am prepared on request to undertake an initial review of any case in which instructing solicitors consider that I may be able to assist. I am prepared to set out in writing how I may be able to help, and to give an indication of my likely fee. In legal aid cases, I will provide a costed programme of work in a form suitable for production by instructing solicitors to the Legal Services Commission for prior authority.

My time spent on that initial review is costed in the fee indicator or the costed programme of work.

If for any reason my potential appointment is not confirmed, there will be no charge for this initial review unless prior agreement on charges has been reached between myself and yourselves, the instructing solicitors.

## Legal aid funded cases

In cases where my fees are to be funded by the Legal Services Commission, I will provide a costed programme of work and require you to obtain its approval (prior authority) by the Legal Services Commission. I wish to receive a copy of the form of approval, before any work is undertaken. I reserve the right to approach the Legal Services Commission through you for prior approval of fees to complete the work, or to undertake additional work, should this prove necessary.

Where a fee has been agreed in advance with the Legal Services Commission or your client, I reserve the right to invoice the full cost of my fees even if this exceeds the fee agreed in advance.

Insert here 1) or 2) below; 1) is more favourable for solicitors but may be necessary for you to secure the work.

1) I will not demand payment of that excess until the conclusion of the case, at which stage all

or part of that excess will be cancelled if it is not recovered by instructing solicitors, at taxation of costs or otherwise.

2) Irrespective of when or indeed if instructing solicitors receive payment from the Legal Services Commission, my fees shall be paid within 14 days of the date of my invoice.

Instructing solicitors will apply promptly to the Legal Services Commission for interim payments of my fees and disbursements as invoiced, and will remit promptly to me all such payments received.

Instructing solicitors will also use their best endeavours to ensure that:

i.    my personal expenses are paid on account;

ii.   where a taxation/assessment of costs is necessary, it will be applied for, pursued or defended (as appropriate) in a timely manner, and that

iii.  my reasonable fees and disbursements are recovered in full by way of the Legal Services Commission.

**Privately funded cases**

In privately funded cases, the instructing solicitors will at all times ensure that they are in funds to discharge and that they do promptly discharge my fees and disbursements [within e.g. 21 days/28 days of date of invoice], unless specifically agreed otherwise. I remind you that you remain liable to pay my invoice even if your client has not paid you. My full fees are to be paid irrespective of the outcome of any taxation of costs.

I reserve the right to charge interest at 3% above Lloyds Bank base rates on overdue amounts.

Once it has been agreed, this letter will remain effective until it is replaced.

I shall be obliged if you will acknowledge acceptance of the terms of this letter by signing the duplicate copy and returning it to me, keeping the first copy with your records.

If the contents are not in accordance with your understanding of our agreement, I shall be pleased to receive your further observations and to give you any further information you require.

Yours faithfully

THE ABOVE TERMS AND CONDITIONS ARE AGREED

    Signed................................

    Position..............................

    Firm..................................

    Date..................................

# MODEL REPORT

*This model report contains references to paragraphs from the Protocol for the Instruction of Experts to give Evidence in Civil Claims. This is reproduced at Appendix 4.*

XXXXXXXX V XXXXXXXX                     XXXXXXXXXX
*[Title of the action]*                        *[Court reference number]*

---

**FINAL REPORT OF** *[your name]* **FOR THE** *[name of the court]*

---

**Dated:** *[The date you sign your report and send it to your instructing solicitors]*

**Specialist field:** *[Your specialist field]*

**On behalf of** *[the Claimant/Defendant (or both if single joint expert)]*: *[The name of the party to the action]*

**On the instructions of:** *[The name of the solicitors who have instructed you]*

**Subject matter:** *[A very brief description of the subject matter]*

*This format is only a **suggestion**. It contains the main elements you will need to consider but you will need to create your own personal format that will depend on your specialist field and the particular case. This front page should be visible, preferably with a transparent plastic sheet, although this is optional. Do not use comb binders. Use A4 good quality paper, hole-punched for lever arch file with a slide binder. Find out from the solicitors who instruct you how many top copies are needed. Your report should be addressed to the court and not to the party from whom you received instructions.*

*[Your]*   **Name:**
       **Address:**
       **Telephone number**
       **Fax number:**
       **Email:**
       **Reference:**

**Report of** *[your name]*                                  *Page 2*
**Specialist field** *[your specialist field]*
**On behalf of** *[the claimant/defendant – name of the party you have been instructed by or Single Joint Expert]*

---

## CONTENTS

| Paragraph number | Paragraph contents | Page number |
|---|---|---|
| 1 | Introduction | |
| 2 | The issues to be addressed and a statement of instructions | |
| 3 | My investigation of the facts | |
| 4 | My opinion | |
| 5 | Statement of compliance | |
| 6 | Statement of truth | |
| 7 | Statement of conflicts | |
| 8 | Declaration | |

*Appendices*

| | | |
|---|---|---|
| 1 | Details of my qualifications and experience | |
| 2 | Experience, qualifications, training of others involved in carrying out any test or experiment | |
| 3 | Statement of methodology | |
| 4 | List of documents that I have examined, with copies of important documents | |
| 5 | Details of any literature or other material I have relied upon in making this report, with copies of important extracts | |
| 6 | Photographs, drawings, schedules, diagrams, graphs and other graphics | |

**Report of** *[your name]*
**Specialist field** *[your specialist field]*
**On behalf of** *[the claimant/defendant – name of the party you have been instructed by or Single Joint Expert]*

---

| 7 | Chronology |
| 8 | Glossary of technical terms |
| 9 | *Other* |

*This contents page is useful even if the report is short. In longer reports, the contents page may need to be more detailed so the reader can easily find their way around the report.*

**Report of** *[your name]* *Page 4*
**Specialist field** *[your specialist field]*
**On behalf of** *[the claimant/defendant – name of the party you have been instructed by or Single Joint Expert]*

---

## REPORT

### 1 Introduction

#### *1.01    The writer*

I am *[your full name]*. My specialist field is *[your specialist field and give a short summary of the most important qualifications and experience relevant to the case – no more than three lines]*.

*(Civil experts: Protocol for the Instruction of Experts to give evidence in civil claims, June 2005 ["Protocol"] paragraph 13.6.)*

*(Criminal experts: R v Bowman paragraph 177, CPS Disclosure Manual Annex K, CrPR 33.3(1)(a).)*

Full details of my qualifications and experience entitling me to give expert opinion evidence are in Appendix 1. *[It is necessary to have these full details as you may be cross-examined on them.]*

#### *1.02    Summary background of the case*

The case concerns *[give a short outline of the case]*. There is a chronology of the key events in Appendix 7. I have been instructed to *[say briefly what you have been asked to do. The purpose of the report should be stated]*.

*(Civil experts: Protocol paragraph 13.15.)*

*(Criminal experts: CPS Disclosure Manual Annex K, CrPR 33.3(1)(h).)*

**Report of** *[your name]*
**Specialist field** *[your specialist field]*
**On behalf of** *[the claimant/defendant – name of the party you have been instructed by or Single Joint Expert]*

---

### 1.03    Summary of my conclusions

This report will show that in my professional opinion *[give your conclusion. It is good practice to put an "executive" summary at the beginning so that the reader knows the direction of your analysis. The Civil Procedure Rules require your report to contain a summary of the conclusions].*

*(Civil experts: Practice Direction 35 paragraph 2.2(7), Protocol paragraph 13.14.)*

*(Criminal experts: CPS Disclosure Manual Annex K, CrPR 33.3(1)(h).)*

### 1.04    The parties involved

Those involved in the case are as follows:

*[List the people and organisations you refer to in your report with a short description of each. This can be very useful for a judge.]*

**Report of** *[your name]*                                                 *Page 6*
**Specialist field** *[your specialist field]*
**On behalf of** *[the claimant/defendant – name of the party you have been instructed
by or Single Joint Expert]*

---

### 1.05    Technical terms and explanations

I have indicated any technical terms in **bold type**. I have defined these terms
when first used and included them in a glossary in Appendix 8. I have also
included in Appendix 5 extracts of published works I refer to in my report
*(Criminal experts: CrPR 33.3(1)(b))* and in Appendix 6 there are diagrams
and photographs to assist in the understanding of the case.

**Report of** *[your name]*                                     *Page 7*
**Specialist field** *[your specialist field]*
**On behalf of** *[the claimant/defendant – name of the party you have been instructed by or Single Joint Expert]*

---

## 2   The issues to be addressed and a statement of instructions

**2.01**   *[Give a statement setting out the substance of all material instructions (whether written or oral, including the questions on which your opinion is sought, the materials provided and considered, and the documents, statements, evidence, information or assumptions are material in your opinion(s). This may be an expanded version of what you say in paragraph 1.02. (Civil experts: Protocol 13.15.)*

*The statement should summarise the facts and instructions given to you which are material to the opinions expressed in your report or upon which these opinions are based. Remember that section 3 will give details of your investigation of the facts. You should make it clear when particular question or issue falls outside your expertise.] (Criminal experts: CrPR 33.3(1)(c), R v Bowman paragraph 177, R v Harris paragraph 271.)*

**2.02**   The purpose of the report.

**2.03**   *[Set out the issues you will address in your report. Number each issue as you will refer to each in your opinion in paragraph 4. Do not give your opinion here.]*

**Report of** *[your name]* Page 8
**Specialist field** *[your specialist field]*
**On behalf of** *[the claimant/defendant – name of the party you have been instructed by or Single Joint Expert]*

---

## 3 My investigation of the facts

- All relevant facts
- Logical order
- Source of facts
- Proper investigations, recording, methodology
- Keep facts separate from opinions

NOTE: LAWYERS WILL CROSS-EXAMINE THE EXPERT WITNESS TO TRY TO DISCREDIT THE SOURCE OF FACTS, METHODOLOGY, DATA, RECORDS, INVESTIGATIONS, CALCULATIONS, ASSUMPTIONS ETC.

*[This section establishes the foundation of fact upon which you will base your opinion. The starting point is "I do not know, but let me see what the facts are". Set out the facts of the case as you see them. Identify the source of these facts. You must distinguish fact from opinion. Also distinguish facts you have been told and those you have personally observed. This paragraph is purely factual. Paragraph 4 will deal with your opinion.]*

*(Criminal experts: CPS Disclosure Manual Annex K, CrPR 33.3(1)(d).)*

### 3.01 Assumed facts

*[State fully the facts that you have been asked to assume. Where the facts are open to more than one interpretation, set out the options and discuss why each interpretation has been rejected or accepted.]*

**Report of** *[your name]*                                      *Page 9*
**Specialist field** *[your specialist field]*
**On behalf of** *[the claimant/defendant – name of the party you have been instructed by or Single Joint Expert]*

---

### 3.02    Enquiries/investigation into facts by the expert

*[Facts established by the expert him/herself in examinations, tests, experiments, calculations, investigations, or inspections should be set out in detail. Be careful to give sufficient explanation of how these facts were obtained and checked to fully discharge your professional obligations and increase credibility as an expert.] (Civil experts: Protocol para 13.7.)*

### 3.03    Documents

*[Identify the important documents for the judge. Remember that Appendix 2 contains a list of the documents (including statements) you have considered with copies of the really important ones.] (Criminal experts: CPS Disclosure Manual Annex K.)*

### 3.04    Interview and examination

*[Give details of any interview and examination you did, including the methodology and/or whether they were carried out under your supervision.] (Criminal experts: R v Bowman, paragraph 177.)*

*[Give dates and times. Say if anyone else was present. There may be none.] (Civil experts.)*

### 3.05    Research

*[Give details of any research papers you considered. Remember that Appendix 5 contains a list of published works you refer to and has copy extracts. Lord Woolf has recommended that, as an expert, you should give details of any literature or other material which you have used in making your report.]*

**Report of** *[your name]*                                                           *Page 10*
**Specialist field** *[your specialist field]*
**On behalf of** *[the claimant/defendant – name of the party you have been instructed*
*by or Single Joint Expert]*

---

### 3.06      Measurements, tests and experiments, etc.

*[You should say who carried out any test or experiment which you use in*
*your report and whether or not the test or experiment has been carried out*
*under supervision. Give the qualifications and experience of the person who*
*carried out any such test or experiment.] (Criminal experts: R v Bowman*
*paragraph 177.) (Civil experts: Protocol paragraph 13.7.)*

### 3.07      Facts obtained by others

*[If tests or experiments have been carried out by someone other than the*
*expert, the report needs to state who did them, provide details of their*
*qualifications and experience and state whether they were carried out under*
*the expert's supervision.] (Civil experts: Practice Direction paragraph*
*2.2(4) and (5).)*

*If the expert's opinion was not formed independently, make it clear from*
*whom the opinion was obtained.] (Civil experts: Protocol para 13.8.)*

**Report of** *[your name]*                                                    *Page 11*
**Specialist field** *[your specialist field]*
**On behalf of** *[the claimant/defendant – name of the party you have been instructed by or Single Joint Expert]*

---

### 4   My opinion

#### *Civil experts*

*[Go through each issue identified in paragraph 2, link these to the facts from paragraph 3 and then give your reasoned arguments for the opinion you come to.*

*Facts, analysis, then argued conclusion. It is useful to use the word "because" to identify why you have come to your opinion. Avoid using the word "negligence" as this is a legal term. Let the judge make the decision; just give your professional opinion. Do not give a legal opinion.*

*Where there is a range of opinion on matters dealt with in your report:*

*i.   summarise the range of opinion, and*

*ii.  give reasons for your opinion.*

*(Practice Direction 35, paragraph 2.2(6).)*

*If there is a range of opinions based on published sources, these should be explained and the expert should indicate how they differ from those opinions. If the opinions are not published, experts may need to explain what they believe to be the range of other experts and make it clear that the range they summarise is based on their own judgment and the basis of that judgment.] (Protocol paragraphs 13.12 and 13.13.)*

**Report of** *[your name]* Page 12
**Specialist field** *[your specialist field]*
**On behalf of** *[the claimant/defendant – name of the party you have been instructed by or Single Joint Expert]*

---

*Criminal experts*

*[Set out any material facts or matters which detract from your opinion and any points which should fairly be made against your opinion.] (R v Bowman paragraph 177.)*

*[If your opinion is not properly researched because you consider that insufficient data is available, this must be stated with an indication that the opinion is no more than a provisional one.] (R v Harris paragraph 271.)*

*[Where you have provided qualified opinion, detail the qualifications.] (CrPR 33.3(g), CPS Disclosure Manual Annex K.)*

*[Where there is a range of opinion on matters dealt with in your report:*

*iii. summarise the range of opinion, and*

*iv. give reasons for your opinion.]*

*(CrPR 33.3(1)(f).)*

*Report of [your name]*          *Page 13*
*Specialist field [your specialist field]*
*On behalf of [the claimant/defendant – name of the party you have been instructed*
*by or Single Joint Expert]*

---

## 5 Statement of compliance (Civil)

I understand my duty as an expert witness is to the court. I have complied with that duty. This report includes all matters relevant to the issues on which my expert evidence is given. I have given details in this report of any matters which might affect the validity of this report. I have addressed this report to the court.

### Statement of compliance (Criminal)

I understand my duty as an expert witness to the court to provide independent assistance by way of objective unbiased opinion in relation to matters within my expertise. I will inform all parties and where appropriate the court in the event that my opinion changes on any material issues (*R v Bowman* paragraph 177, CrPR 33.3(1)(i)).

## 6 Statement of truth (Civil)

I confirm that insofar as the facts stated in my report are within my own knowledge, I have made clear which they are and I believe them to be true, and that the opinions I have expressed represent my true and complete professional opinion.

*(Practice Direction 35 paragraph 2.2(9). Also, note the Protocol paragraph 13.5 which states that the wording is mandatory and should not be modified.)*

*(Please note Rule 32.14 which sets out the consequences of verifying a document containing a false statement without an honest belief in its truth. For information about statements of truth, see Part 22 of the Rules and the practice direction which supplements them.)*

**Report of** *[your name]*                                     *Page 14*
**Specialist field** *[your specialist field]*
**On behalf of** *[the claimant/defendant – name of the party you have been instructed by or Single Joint Expert]*

---

### 7   Statement of conflicts

I confirm that I have no conflict of interest of any kind, other than any which I have set out in this report. I do not consider that any interest which I have disclosed affects my suitability to give expert evidence on any issue on which I have given evidence and I will advise the party by whom I am instructed if, between the date of this report and the trial, there is any change in circumstances which affects this statement.

*[This statement of conflicts is not mandatory but is suggested in the judgment of Sir Mark Potter in Toth v Jarman [2006] EWCA Civ 1028 paragraph 120. He also urged the Civil Procedure Rules Committee to consider including it in the CPR.]*

**Specialist field** *[your specialist field]*
**On behalf of** *[the claimant/defendant – name of the party you have been instructed by or Single Joint Expert]*

---

## 8   Declaration (Criminal)

This statement consisting of [XXX] pages each signed by me, is true to the best of my knowledge and belief and I make it knowing that, if it is tendered in evidence, I shall be liable to prosecution if I have wilfully stated in it anything which I know to be false or do not believe to be true.

**Signature** ........................................................ **Date** ....................................

*[Do not forget to sign and date your report!]*

**Report of** *[your name]* Page 16
**Specialist field** *[your specialist field]*
**On behalf of** *[the claimant/defendant – name of the party you have been instructed by or Single Joint Expert]*

***Specialist field** [your specialist field]*
***On behalf of** [the claimant/defendant – name of the party you have been instructed
by or Single Joint Expert]*

## Appendix 1

### *Details of my qualifications and experience*

*This is the front sheet for the contents of the Appendix. Have a separate
sheet for each appendix, unless it is a very short report.*

## HERE IS A CHECK LIST TO USE WHEN YOU HAVE
## COMPLETED YOUR REPORT

**yes**    **no**
✓      ✓

❑   ❑  A4 good quality paper, hole punched for lever arch file

❑   ❑  Quality printing

❑   ❑  Chronology

❑   ❑  Clear headings

❑   ❑  Contents page

❑   ❑  Covering letter and invoice

❑   ❑  Dated

❑   ❑  Declarations included

❑   ❑  Double spaced or space and a half

❑   ❑  Expressed in the first person

❑   ❑  Front sheet

❑   ❑  Glossary

❑   ❑  Graphics

❑   ❑  Headers on each page

❑   ❑  Margins wide enough for written comments

❑   ❑  Pages numbered

❑   ❑  Paragraphs numbered

❑   ❑  Publications dated and precede incident date (if appropriate)

❑   ❑  Short sentences and paragraphs

❑   ❑  Signed

❑   ❑  Synopsis

**Review the following pointers:**

✓

❑   Accurate?

❑   Clear conclusion?

❑   Fact and opinion clearly separated?

❑   Good use of appendices?

❑   How concise is the report?

❑   How clearly are the issues identified?

❑   How clear is the language for a non expert to read?

❑   How logical is the report?

❑   How far does the report stand alone, i.e. contains everything that the judge would need?

❑   How well are the qualifications and experience set out?

❑   *EASY for judges and lawyers to use?!*

## Appendix 3

# CIVIL PROCEDURE RULES 1998 – PART 35 AND PRACTICE DIRECTION

## PART 35 – EXPERTS AND ASSESSORS

*Duty to restrict expert evidence*

35.1 Expert evidence shall be restricted to that which is reasonably required to resolve the proceedings.

*Interpretation*

35.2 A reference to an 'expert' in this Part is a reference to an expert who has been instructed to give or prepare evidence for the purpose of court proceedings.

*Experts – overriding duty to the court*

35.3 1. It is the duty of an expert to help the court on the matters within his expertise.

2. This duty overrides any obligation to the person from whom he has received instructions or by whom he is paid.

*Court's power to restrict expert evidence*

35.4 1. No party may call an expert or put in evidence an expert's report without the court's permission.

2. When a party applies for permission under this rule he must identify –

a. the field in which he wishes to rely on expert evidence; and

b. where practicable the expert in that field on whose evidence he wishes to rely.

3. If permission is granted under this rule it shall be in relation only to the expert named or the field identified under paragraph (2).

4. The court may limit the amount of the expert's fees and expenses that the party who wishes to rely on the expert may recover from any other party.

*General requirement for expert evidence to be given in a written report*

35.5 1. Expert evidence is to be given in a written report unless the court directs otherwise.

2. If a claim is on the fast track, the court will not direct an expert to attend a hearing unless it is necessary to do so in the interests of justice.

*Written questions to experts*

35.6 1. A party may put to –

a. an expert instructed by another party; or

b. a single joint expert appointed under rule 35.7,

written questions about his report.

2. Written questions under paragraph (1) –

a. may be put once only;

b. must be put within 28 days of service of the expert's report; and

c. must be for the purpose only of clarification of the report,

unless in any case –

i. the court gives permission; or

    ii. the other party agrees.

3. An expert's answers to questions put in accordance with paragraph (1) shall be treated as part of the expert's report.

4. Where –

    a. a party has put a written question to an expert instructed by another party in accordance with this rule; and

    b. the expert does not answer that question,

    the court may make one or both of the following orders in relation to the party who instructed the expert –

    i. that the party may not rely on the evidence of that expert; or

    ii. that the party may not recover the fees and expenses of that expert from any other party.

*Court's power to direct that evidence is to be given by a single joint expert*

35.7 1. Where two or more parties wish to submit expert evidence on a particular issue, the court may direct that the evidence on that issue is to given by one expert only.

2. The parties wishing to submit the expert evidence are called 'the instructing parties'.

3. Where the instructing parties cannot agree who should be the expert, the court may –

    a. select the expert from a list prepared or identified by the instructing parties; or

    b. direct that the expert be selected in such other manner as the court may direct.

*Instructions to a single joint expert*

35.8  1.  Where the court gives a direction under rule 35.7 for a single joint expert to be used, each instructing party may give instructions to the expert.

2.  When an instructing party gives instructions to the expert he must, at the same time, send a copy of the instructions to the other instructing parties.

3.  The court may give directions about –

a.  the payment of the expert's fees and expenses; and

b.  any inspection, examination or experiments which the expert wishes to carry out.

4.  The court may, before an expert is instructed –

a.  limit the amount that can be paid by way of fees and expenses to the expert; and

b.  direct that the instructing parties pay that amount into court.

5.  Unless the court otherwise directs, the instructing parties are jointly and severally liable (GL) for the payment of the expert's fees and expenses.

*Power of court to direct a party to provide information*

35.9  Where a party has access to information which is not reasonably available to the other party, the court may direct the party who has access to the information to –

a.  prepare and file a document recording the information; and

b.  serve a copy of that document on the other party.

*Contents of report*

35.10 1. An expert's report must comply with the requirements set out in the relevant practice direction.

2. At the end of an expert's report there must be a statement that –

a. the expert understands his duty to the court; and

b. he has complied with that duty.

3. The expert's report must state the substance of all material instructions, whether written or oral, on the basis of which the report was written.

4. The instructions referred to in paragraph (3) shall not be privileged (GL) against disclosure but the court will not, in relation to those instructions –

a. order disclosure of any specific document; or

b. permit any questioning in court, other than by the party who instructed the expert,

unless it is satisfied that there are reasonable grounds to consider the statement of instructions given under paragraph (3) to be inaccurate or incomplete.

*Use by one party of expert's report disclosed by another*

35.11 Where a party has disclosed an expert's report, any party may use that expert's report as evidence at the trial.

*Discussions between experts*

35.12 1. The court may, at any stage, direct a discussion between experts for the purpose of requiring the experts to –

a. identify and discuss the expert issues in the proceedings; and

b. where possible, reach an agreed opinion on those issues.

2. The court may specify the issues which the experts must discuss.

3. The court may direct that following a discussion between the experts they must prepare a statement for the court showing –

   a. those issues on which they agree; and

   b. those issues on which they disagree and a summary of their reasons for disagreeing.

4. The content of the discussion between the experts shall not be referred to at the trial unless the parties agree.

5. Where experts reach agreement on an issue during their discussions, the agreement shall not bind the parties unless the parties expressly agree to be bound by the agreement.

*Consequence of failure to disclose expert's report*

35.13 A party who fails to disclose an expert's report may not use the report at the trial or call the expert to give evidence orally unless the court gives permission.

*Expert's right to ask court for directions*

35.14 1. An expert may file a written request for directions to assist him in carrying out his function as an expert.

2. An expert must, unless the court orders otherwise, provide a copy of any proposed request for directions under paragraph (1)–

   a. to the party instructing him, at least 7 days before he files the request; and

b. to all other parties, at least 4 days before he files it.

3. The court, when it gives directions, may also direct that a party be served with a copy of the directions.

*Assessors*

35.15 1. This rule applies where the court appoints one or more persons (an 'assessor') under section 70 of the Supreme Court Act 1981 or section 63 of the County Courts Act 1984.

2. The assessor shall assist the court in dealing with a matter in which the assessor has skill and experience.

3. An assessor shall take such part in the proceedings as the court may direct and in particular the court may –

a. direct the assessor to prepare a report for the court on any matter at issue in the proceedings; and

b. direct the assessor to attend the whole or any part of the trial to advise the court on any such matter.

4. If the assessor prepares a report for the court before the trial has begun –

a. the court will send a copy to each of the parties; and

b. the parties may use it at trial.

5. The remuneration to be paid to the assessor for his services shall be determined by the court and shall form part of the costs of the proceedings.

6. The court may order any party to deposit in the court office a specified sum in respect of the assessor's fees and, where it does so, the assessor will not be asked to act until the sum has been deposited.

7. Paragraphs (5) and (6) do not apply where the remuneration of the assessor is to be paid out of money provided by Parliament.

## PRACTICE DIRECTION – EXPERTS AND ASSESSORS, PART 35

Part 35 is intended to limit the use of oral expert evidence to that which is reasonably required. In addition, where possible, matters requiring expert evidence should be dealt with by a single expert. Permission of the court is always required either to call an expert or to put an expert's report in evidence. There is annexed to this Practice Direction a protocol for the instruction of experts to give evidence in civic claims. Experts and those instructing them are expected to have regard to the guidance contained in the protocol.

*Expert Evidence – General Requirements*

1.1    It is the duty of an exper to help the court on matter within his own expertise: rule 35.3(1). This duty is paramount and overrides any obligation to the person from whom the expert has received instuctions or by whom he is paid: rule 35.3(2).

1.2    Expert evidence should be the independent product of the expert uninfluenced by the pressures of litigation.

1.3    An expert should assist the court by providing objective unbiased opinion on matters within his expertise and should not assume the role of an advocate.

1.4    An expert should consider all material facts, including those which might detract from his opinion

1.5    An expert should make it clear:

   a. when a question or issue falls outside his expertise; and

b. when he is not able to reach a definite opinion, for example because he has insufficientt information.

1.6    If, after producing a report, an expert changes his view on any material matter, such change of view should be communicated to all parties without delay, and when appropriate to the court.

*Form and content of expert's reports*

2.1    An expert's report should be addressed to the court and not to the party from whom the expert has received his instructions.

2.2    An expert's report must:

1. give details of the expert's qualifications;

2. give details of any literature or other material which the expert has relied on in making the report;

3. contain a statement setting out the substance of all facts and instructions given to the expert which are material to the opinions expressed in the report or upon which those opinions are based;

4. make clear which facts stated in the report are within the expert's own knowledge;

5. say who carried out any examination, measurement, test or experiment which the expert has used for the report and whether or not the test or experiment has been carried out under the expert's supervision;

6. where there is a range of opinion on the matters dealt within the report:

    i.    summarise the range of opinion, and

    ii.   give reasons for his own opinion;

7. contain a summary of the conclusions reached;

8. if the expert is not able to give his opinion without qualification, state that qualification; and

9. contain a statement that the expert understands his duty to the court, and has complied with and will continue to comply that duty

2.3    An expert's report must be verified by a statement of truth as well as containing the statements required in paragraph 2.2(8) and (9) above.

2.4    The form of the statement of truth is as follows: "I confirm that insofar as the facts stated in my report are within my own knowledge, I have made clear which they are and I believe them to be true, and that the opinions I have expressed represent my true and complete professional opinion".

2.5    Attention is drawn to rule 32.14 which sets out the consequences of verifying a document containing a false statement without an honest belief in its truth. (For information about statements of truth see Part 22 and the Practice Direction which supplements it.)

*Information*

3.    Under rule 35.9 the court may direct a party with access to information which is not reasonably available to another party, to serve on that other party a document which records the information. The document served must include sufficient details of any facts, tests, experiments and assumptions which underline any part of the information to enable the party on whom it is served to make, or to obtain a proper interpretation of the information and an assessment of its significance.

*Instructions*

4.    The instructions referred to in paragraph 2.2(3) will not be
      protected by privilege (see rule 35.10(4)). But cross-examination
      of the expert on the contents of his instructions will not be
      allowed unless the court permits it (or unless the party who
      gave the instructions consents to it). Before it gives permission
      the court must be satisfied that there are reasonable grounds
      to consider that the statement in the report of the substance of
      the instructions is inaccurate or incomplete. If the court is so
      satisfied, it will allow the cross-examination where it appears to
      be in the interests of justice to do so.

*Questions to experts*

5.1   Questions asked for the purpose of clarifying the expert's report
      (see rule 35.6) should be put, in writing, to the expert not later
      than 28 days after receipt of the expert's report (see paragraphs
      1.2 to 1.5 above as to verification).

5.2   Where a party sends a written question or questions direct to
      an expert, a copy of the questions should, at the same time, be
      sent to the other party or parties.

5.3   The party or parties instructing the expert must pay any fees
      charged by that expert for answering questions put under rule
      35.6. This does not affect any decision of the court as to the
      party who is ultimately to bear the expert's costs.

*Single expert*

6.    Where the court has directed that the evidence on a particular
      issue is to be given by one expert only (rule 35.7) but there are
      a number of disciplines relevant to that issue, a leading expert
      in the dominant discipline should be identified as the single
      expert. He should prepare the general part of the report and be

responsible for annexing or incorporating the contents of any reports from experts in other disciplines.

## Orders

6A.    Where an order requires an act to be done by an expert, or otherwise affects an expert, the party instructing that expert must serve a copy of the order ont he expert instructed by him. In the case of a jointly instructed expert, the claimant must serve the order.

## Assessors

7.1    An assessor may be appointed to assist the court under rule 35.15. Not less than 21 days before making any such appointment, the court will notify each party in writing of the name of the proposed assessor, of the matter in respect of which the assistance of the assessor will be sought and of the qualifications of the assessor to give that assistance.

7.2    Where any person has been proposed for appointment as an assessor, objection to him, either personally or in respect of his qualification, may be taken by any party.

7.3    Any such objection must be made in writing and filed with the court within 7 days of receipt of the notification referred to in paragraph 6.1 and will be taken into account by the court in deciding whether or not to make the appointment (section 63(5) of the County Courts Act 1984).

7.4    Copies of any report prepared by the assessor will be sent to each of the parties but the assessor will not give oral evidence or be open to cross-examination or questioning.

# PROTOCOL FOR THE INSTRUCTION OF EXPERTS TO GIVE EVIDENCE IN CIVIL CLAIMS
## An Annex to the Practice Direction to Part 35

## Introduction

1.1     Expert witnesses perform a vital role in civil litigation. It is essential that both those who instruct experts and experts themselves are given clear guidance as to what they are expected to do in civil proceedings. The purpose of this Protocol is to provide such guidance. It has been drafted by the Civil Justice Council and reflects the rules and practice directions current [in June 2005], replacing the Code of Guidance on Expert Evidence. The authors of the Protocol wish to acknowledge the valuable assistance they obtained by drawing on earlier documents produced by the Academy of Experts and the Expert Witness Institute, as well as suggestions made by the Clinical Dispute Forum. The Protocol has been approved by the Master of the Rolls.

### Aims of Protocol

2.1     This Protocol offers guidance to experts and to those instructing them in the interpretation of and compliance with Part 35 of the Civil Procedure Rules (CPR 35) and its associated Practice Direction (PD 35) and to further the objectives of the Civil Procedure Rules in general. It is intended to assist in the interpretation of those provisions in the interests of good practice but it does not replace them. It sets out standards for the use of experts and the conduct of experts and those who instruct them. The existence of this Protocol does not remove the need for experts and those who instruct them to be familiar with CPR 35 and PD 35.

2.2   Experts and those who instruct them should also bear in mind paragraph 1.4 of the Practice Direction on Protocols which contains the following objectives, namely to:

a. encourage the exchange of early and full information about the expert issues involved in a prospective legal claim;

b. enable the parties to avoid or reduce the scope of litigation by agreeing the whole or part of an expert issue before commencement of proceedings; and

c  support the efficient management of proceedings where litigation cannot be avoided.

## Application

3.1   This Protocol applies to any steps taken for the purpose of civil proceedings by experts or those who instruct them on or after 5th September 2005.

3.2   It applies to all experts who are, or who may be, governed by CPR Part 35 and to those who instruct them. Experts are governed by Part 35 if they are or have been instructed to give or prepare evidence for the purpose of civil proceedings in a court in England and Wales (CPR 35.2).

3.3   Experts, and those instructing them, should be aware that some cases may be "specialist proceedings" (CPR 49) where there are modifications to the Civil Procedure Rules. Proceedings may also be governed by other Protocols. Further, some courts have published their own Guides which supplement the Civil Procedure Rules for proceedings in those courts. They contain provisions affecting expert evidence. Expert witnesses and those instructing them should be familiar with them when they are relevant.

3.4     Courts may take into account any failure to comply with this Protocol when making orders in relation to costs, interest, time limits, the stay of proceedings and whether to order a party to pay a sum of money into court.

*Limitation*

3.5     If, as a result of complying with any part of this Protocol, claims would or might be time barred under any provision in the Limitation Act 1980, or any other legislation that imposes a time limit for the bringing an action, claimants may commence proceedings without complying with this Protocol. In such circumstances, claimants who commence proceedings without complying with all, or any part, of this. Protocol must apply, giving notice to all other parties, to the court for directions as to the timetable and form of procedure to be adopted, at the same time as they request the court to issue proceedings. The court may consider whether to order a stay of the whole or part of the proceedings pending compliance with this Protocol and may make orders in relation to costs.

## Duties of experts

4.1     Experts always owe a duty to exercise reasonable skill and care to those instructing them, and to comply with any relevant professional code of ethics. However when they are instructed to give or prepare evidence for the purpose of civil proceedings in England and Wales they have an overriding duty to help the court on matters within their expertise (CPR 35.3). This duty overrides any obligation to the person instructing or paying them. Experts must not serve the exclusive interest of those who retain them.

4.2   Experts should be aware of the overriding objective that courts deal with cases justly. This includes dealing with cases proportionately, expeditiously and fairly (CPR 1.1). Experts are under an obligation to assist the court so as to enable them to deal with cases in accordance with the overriding objective. However the overriding objective does not impose on experts any duty to act as mediators between the parties or require them to trespass on the role of the court in deciding facts.

4.3   Experts should provide opinions which are independent, regardless of the pressures of litigation. In this context, a useful test of 'independence' is that the expert would express the same opinion if given the same instructions by an opposing party. Experts should not take it upon themselves to promote the point of view of the party instructing them or engage in the role of advocates.

4.4   Experts should confine their opinions to matters which are material to the disputes between the parties and provide opinions only in relation to matters which lie within their expertise. Experts should indicate without delay where particular questions or issues fall outside their expertise.

4.5   Experts should take into account all material facts before them at the time that they give their opinion. Their reports should set out those facts and any literature or any other material on which they have relied in forming their opinions. They should indicate if an opinion is provisional, or qualified, or where they consider that further information is required or if, for any other reason, they are not satisfied that an opinion can be expressed finally and without qualification.

4.6 Experts should inform those instructing them without delay of any change in their opinions on any material matter and the reason for it.

4.7 Experts should be aware that any failure by them to comply with the Civil Procedure Rules or court orders or any excessive delay for which they are responsible may result in the parties who instructed them being penalised in costs and even, in extreme cases, being debarred from placing the experts' evidence before the court. In *Phillips v Symes*[1] Peter Smith J held that courts may also make orders for costs (under section 51 of the Supreme Court Act 1981) directly against expert witnesses who by their evidence cause significant expense to be incurred, and do so in flagrant and reckless disregard of their duties to the Court.

## Conduct of experts instructed only to advise

5.1 Part 35 only applies where experts are instructed to give opinions which are relied on for the purposes of court proceedings. Advice which the parties do not intend to adduce in litigation is likely to be confidential; the Protocol does not apply in these circumstances.[2][3]

5.2 The same applies where, after the commencement of proceedings, experts are instructed only to advise (e.g. to

---

[1] *Phillips v Symes* [2004] EWHC 2330 (Ch).

[2] *Carlson v Townsend* [2001] 1 WLR 2415.

[3] *Jackson v Marley Davenport* [2004] 1 WLR 2926.

comment upon a single joint expert's report) and not to give or prepare evidence for use in the proceedings.

5.3    However this Protocol does apply if experts who were formerly instructed only to advise are later instructed to give or prepare evidence for the purpose of civil proceedings.

## The Need for Experts

6.1    Those intending to instruct experts to give or prepare evidence for the purpose of civil proceedings should consider whether expert evidence is appropriate, taking account of the principles set out in CPR Parts 1 and 35, and in particular whether:

a.  it is relevant to a matter which is in dispute between the parties;

b.  it is reasonably required to resolve the proceedings (CPR 35.1);

c.  the expert has expertise relevant to the issue on which an opinion is sought;

d.  the expert has the experience, expertise and training appropriate to the value, complexity and importance of the case; and

e.  these objects can be achieved by the appointment of a single joint expert (see section 17 below).

6.2    Although the court's permission is not generally required to instruct an expert, the court's permission is required before experts can be called to give evidence or their evidence can be put in (CPR 35.4).

**The appointment of experts**

7.1 Before experts are formally instructed or the court's permission to appoint named experts is sought, the following should be established:

a. that they have the appropriate expertise and experience;

b. that they are familiar with the general duties of an expert;

c. that they can produce a report, deal with questions and have discussions with other experts within a reasonable time and at a cost proportionate to the matters in issue;

d. a description of the work required;

e. whether they are available to attend the trial, if attendance is required; and

f. there is no potential conflict of interest.

7.2 Terms of appointment should be agreed at the outset and should normally include:

a. the capacity in which the expert is to be appointed (e.g. party appointed expert, single joint expert or expert advisor);

b. the services required of the expert (e.g. provision of expert's report, answering questions in writing, attendance at meetings and attendance at court);

c. time for delivery of the report;

d. the basis of the expert's charges (either daily or hourly rates and an estimate of the time likely to be required, or a total fee for the services);

e. travelling expenses and disbursements;

    f.  cancellation charges;

    g.  any fees for attending court;

    h.  time for making the payment;

    i.  whether fees are to be paid by a third party; and

    j.  if a party is publicly funded, whether or not the expert's charges will be subject to assessment by a costs officer.

7.3    As to the appointment of single joint experts, see section 17 below.

7.4    When necessary, arrangements should be made for dealing with questions to experts and discussions between experts, including any directions given by the court, and provision should be made for the cost of this work.

7.5    Experts should be informed regularly about deadlines for all matters concerning them. Those instructing experts should promptly send them copies of all court orders and directions which may affect the preparation of their reports or any other matters concerning their obligations.

*Conditional and Contingency Fees*

7.6    Payments contingent upon the nature of the expert evidence given in legal proceedings, or upon the outcome of a case, must not be offered or accepted. To do so would contravene experts' overriding duty to the court and compromise their duty of independence.

7.7    Agreement to delay payment of experts' fees until after the conclusion of cases is permissible as long as the amount of the fee does not depend on the outcome of the case.

**Instructions**

8.1 Those instructing experts should ensure that they give clear instructions, including the following:

    a. basic information, such as names, addresses, telephone numbers, dates of birth and dates of incidents;

    b. the nature and extent of the expertise which is called for;

    c. the purpose of requesting the advice or report, a description of the matter(s) to be investigated, the principal known issues and the identity of all parties;

    d. the statement(s) of case (if any), those documents which form part of standard disclosure and witness statements which are relevant to the advice or report;

    e. where proceedings have not been started, whether proceedings are being contemplated and, if so, whether the expert is asked only for advice;

    f. an outline programme, consistent with good case management and the expert's availability, for the completion and delivery of each stage of the expert's work; and

    g. where proceedings have been started, the dates of any hearings (including any Case Management Conferences and/or Pre-Trial Reviews), the name of the court, the claim number and the track to which the claim has been allocated.

8.2 Experts who do not receive clear instructions should request clarification and may indicate that they are not prepared to act unless and until such clear instructions are received.

8.3 As to the instruction of single joint experts, see section 17 below.

## Experts' Acceptance of Instructions

9.1 Experts should confirm without delay whether or not they accept instructions. They should also inform those instructing them (whether on initial instruction or at any later stage) without delay if:

    a. instructions are not acceptable because, for example, they require work that falls outside their expertise, impose unrealistic deadlines, or are insufficiently clear;

    b. they consider that instructions are or have become insufficient to complete the work;

    c. they become aware that they may not be able to fulfil any of the terms of appointment;

    d. the instructions and/or work have, for any reason, placed them in conflict with their duties as an expert; or

    e. they are not satisfied that they can comply with any orders that have been made.

9.2 Experts must neither express an opinion outside the scope of their field of expertise, nor accept any instructions to do so.

## Withdrawal

10.1 Where experts' instructions remain incompatible with their duties, whether through incompleteness, a conflict between their duty to the court and their instructions, or for any other substantial and significant reason, they may consider withdrawing from the case. However, experts should not withdraw without first discussing the position fully with those who instruct them and considering carefully whether it would be more appropriate to make a written request for directions from the court. If experts do withdraw, they must give formal written notice to those instructing them.

## Experts' Right to ask Court for Directions

11.1   Experts may request directions from the court to assist them in carrying out their functions as experts. Experts should normally discuss such matters with those who instruct them before making any such request. Unless the court otherwise orders, any proposed request for directions should be copied to the party instructing the expert at least seven days before filing any request to the court, and to all other parties at least four days before filing it (CPR 35.14).

11.2   Requests to the court for directions should be made by letter, containing.

   a.  the title of the claim;

   b.  the claim number of the case;

   c.  the name of the expert;

   d.  full details of why directions are sought; and

   e.  copies of any relevant documentation.

## Power of the Court to Direct a Party to Provide Information

12.1   If experts consider that those instructing them have not provided information which they require, they may, after discussion with those instructing them and giving notice, write to the court to seek directions (CPR 35.14).

12.2   Experts and those who instruct them should also be aware of CPR 35.9. This provides that where one party has access to information which is not readily available to the other party, the court may direct the party who has access to the information to prepare, file and copy to the other party a document recording the information. If experts require such information which has not been disclosed, they should discuss the position with those instructing them without delay, so that a request for the information can be made, and, if not forthcoming, an application can be made to the court. Unless a document appears to be essential, experts should assess the cost and time involved in the production of a document and whether its provision would be proportionate in the context of the case.

## Contents of Experts' Reports

13.1 The content and extent of experts' reports should be governed by the scope of their instructions and general obligations, the contents of CPR 35 and PD 35 and their overriding duty to the court.

13.2 In preparing reports, experts should maintain professional objectivity and impartiality at all times.

13.3 PD 35, paragraph 2, provides that experts' reports should be addressed to the court and gives detailed directions about the form and content of such reports. All experts and those who instruct them should ensure that they are familiar with these requirements.

13.4 Model forms of Experts' Reports are available from bodies such as the Academy of Experts or the Expert Witness Institute.

13.5 Experts' reports must contain statements that they understand their duty to the court and have complied and will continue to comply with that duty (PD 35 paragraph 2.2(9)). They must also be verified by a statement of truth. The form of the statement of truth is as follows: "I confirm that insofar as the facts stated in my report are within my own knowledge I have made clear which they are and I believe them to be true, and that the opinions I have expressed represent my true and complete professional opinion". This wording is mandatory and must not be modified.

*Qualifications*

13.6 The details of experts' qualifications to be given in reports should be commensurate with the nature and complexity of the case. It may be sufficient merely to state academic and professional qualifications. However, where highly specialised expertise is called for, experts should include the detail of particular training and/or experience that qualifies them to provide that highly specialised evidence.

*Tests*

13.7 Where tests of a scientific or technical nature have been carried out, experts should state:

a. the methodology used; and

b. by whom the tests were undertaken and under whose supervision, summarising their respective qualifications and experience.

*Reliance on the work of others*

13.8 Where experts rely in their reports on literature or other material and cite the opinions of others without having verified them, they must give details of those opinions relied on. It is likely to assist the court if the qualifications of the originator(s) are also stated.

*Facts*

13.9 When addressing questions of fact and opinion, experts should keep the two separate and discrete.

13.10 Experts must state those facts (whether assumed or otherwise) upon which their opinions are based. They must distinguish clearly between those facts which experts know to be true and those facts which they assume.

13.11 Where there are material facts in dispute experts should express separate opinions on each hypothesis put forward. They should not express a view in favour of one or other disputed version of the facts unless, as a result of particular expertise and experience, they consider one set of facts as being improbable or less probable, in which case they may express that view, and should give reasons for holding it.

*Range of opinion*

13.12 If the mandatory summary of the range of opinion is based on published sources, experts should explain those sources and, where appropriate, state the qualifications of the originator(s) of the opinions from which they differ, particularly if such opinions represent a well-established school of thought.

13.13 Where there is no available source for the range of opinion, experts may need to express opinions on what they believe to be the range which other experts would arrive at if asked. In those circumstances, experts should make it clear that the range that they summarise is based on their own judgement and explain the basis of that judgement.

*Conclusions*

13.14 A summary of conclusions is mandatory. The summary should be at the end of the report after all the reasoning. There may be cases, however, where the benefit to the court is heightened by placing a short summary at the beginning of the report whilst giving the full conclusions at the end. For example, it can assist with the comprehension of the analysis and with the absorption of the detailed facts if the court is told at the outset of the direction in which the report's logic will flow in cases involving highly complex matters which fall outside the general knowledge of the court.

*Basis of report: material instructions*

13.15 The mandatory statement of the substance of all material instructions should not be incomplete or otherwise tend to mislead. The imperative is transparency. The term "instructions" includes all material which solicitors place in front of experts in order to gain advice. The omission from the statement of 'off-the-record' oral instructions is not permitted. Courts may allow cross-examination about the instructions if there are reasonable grounds to consider that the statement may be inaccurate or incomplete.

## After receipt of experts' reports

14.1 Following the receipt of experts' reports, those instructing them should advise the experts as soon as reasonably practicable whether, and if so when, the report will be disclosed to other parties; and, if so disclosed, the date of actual disclosure.

14.2 If experts' reports are to be relied upon, and if experts are to give oral evidence, those instructing them should give the experts the opportunity to consider and comment upon other reports within their area of expertise and which deal with relevant issues at the earliest opportunity.

14.3 Those instructing experts should keep experts informed of the progress of cases, including amendments to statements of case relevant to experts' opinion.

14.4 If those instructing experts become aware of material changes in circumstances or that relevant information within their control was not previously provided to experts, they should without delay instruct experts to review, and if necessary, update the contents of their reports.

## Amendment of reports

15.1 It may become necessary for experts to amend their reports:

a. as a result of an exchange of questions and answers;

b. following agreements reached at meetings between experts; or

c. where further evidence or documentation is disclosed.

15.2 Experts should not be asked to, and should not, amend, expand or alter any parts of reports in a manner which distorts their true opinion, but may be invited to amend or expand reports to ensure accuracy, internal consistency, completeness and relevance to the issues and clarity. Although experts should generally follow the recommendations of solicitors with regard to the form of reports, they should form their own independent views as to the opinions and contents expressed in their reports and exclude any suggestions which do not accord with their views.

15.3 Where experts change their opinion following a meeting of experts, a simple signed and dated addendum or memorandum to that effect is generally sufficient. In some cases, however, the benefit to the court of having an amended report may justify the cost of making the amendment.

15.4 Where experts significantly alter their opinion, as a result of new evidence or because evidence on which they relied has become unreliable, or for any other reason, they should amend their reports to reflect that fact. Amended reports should include reasons for amendments. In such circumstances those instructing experts should inform other parties as soon as possible of any change of opinion.

15.5   When experts intend to amend their reports, they should inform those instructing them without delay and give reasons. They should provide the amended version (or an addendum or memorandum) clearly marked as such as quickly as possible.

**Written Questions to Experts**

16.1   The procedure for putting written questions to experts (CPR 35.6) is intended to facilitate the clarification of opinions and issues after experts' reports have been served. Experts have a duty to provide answers to questions properly put. Where they fail to do so, the court may impose sanctions against the party instructing the expert and, if there is continued non-compliance, debar a party from relying on the report. Experts should copy their answers to those instructing them.

16.2   Experts' answers to questions automatically become part of their reports. They are covered by the statement of truth and form part of the expert evidence.

16.3   Where experts believe that questions put are not properly directed to the clarification of the report, or are disproportionate, or have been asked out of time, they should discuss the questions with those instructing them and, if appropriate, those asking the questions. Attempts should be made to resolve such problems without the need for an application to the court for directions.

*Written requests for directions in relation to questions*

16.4    If those instructing experts do not apply to the court in respect of questions, but experts still believe that questions are improper or out of time, experts may file written requests with the court for directions to assist in carrying out their functions as experts (CPR 35.14). See Section 11 above.

## Single Joint Experts

17.1    CPR 35 and PD 35 deal extensively with the instruction and use of joint experts by the parties and the powers of the court to order their use (see CPR 35.7 and 35.8, PD 35, paragraph 5).

17.2    The Civil Procedure Rules encourage the use of joint experts. Wherever possible a joint report should be obtained. Consideration should therefore be given by all parties to the appointment of single joint experts in all cases where a court might direct such an appointment. Single joint experts are the norm in cases allocated to the small claims track and the fast track.

17.3    Where, in the early stages of a dispute, examinations, investigations, tests, site inspections, experiments, preparation of photographs, plans or other similar preliminary expert tasks are necessary, consideration should be given to the instruction of a single joint expert, especially where such matters are not, at that stage, expected to be contentious as between the parties. The objective of such an appointment should be to agree or to narrow issues.

17.4    Experts who have previously advised a party (whether in the same case or otherwise) should only be proposed as single joint experts if other parties are given all relevant information about the previous involvement.

17.5   The appointment of a single joint expert does not prevent parties from instructing their own experts to advise (but the costs of such expert advisers may not be recoverable in the case).

*Joint instructions*

17.6   The parties should try to agree joint instructions to single joint experts, but, in default of agreement, each party may give instructions. In particular, all parties should try to agree what documents should be included with instructions and what assumptions single joint experts should make.

17.7   Where the parties fail to agree joint instructions, they should try to agree where the areas of disagreement lie and their instructions should make this clear. If separate instructions are given, they should be copied at the same time to the other instructing parties.

17.8.   Where experts are instructed by two or more parties, the terms of appointment should, unless the court has directed otherwise, or the parties have agreed otherwise, include:

a.   a statement that all the instructing parties are jointly and severally liable to pay the experts' fees and, accordingly, that experts' invoices should be sent simultaneously to all instructing parties or their solicitors (as appropriate); and

b.   a statement as to whether any order has been made limiting the amount of experts' fees and expenses (CPR 35.8(4)(a)).

17.9   Where instructions have not been received by the expert from one or more of the instructing parties the expert should give notice (normally at least 7 days) of a deadline to all instructing parties for the receipt by the expert of such instructions. Unless the instructions are received within the deadline the expert may begin work. In the event that instructions are received after the deadline but before the signing off of the report the expert should consider whether it is practicable to comply with those instructions without adversely affecting the timetable set for delivery of the report and in such a manner as to comply with the proportionality principle. An expert who decides to issue a report without taking into account instructions received after the deadline should inform the parties who may apply to the court for directions. In either event the report must show clearly that the expert did not receive instructions within the deadline, or, as the case may be, at all.

*Conduct of the single joint expert*

17.10 Single joint experts should keep all instructing parties informed of any material steps that they may be taking by, for example, copying all correspondence to those instructing them.

17.11 Single joint experts are Part 35 experts and so have an overriding duty to the court. They are the parties' appointed experts and therefore owe an equal duty to all parties. They should maintain independence, impartiality and transparency at all times.

17.12 Single joint experts should not attend any meeting or conference which is not a joint one, unless all the parties have agreed in writing or the court has directed that such a meeting may be held[1] and who is to pay the experts' fees for the meeting.

17.13 Single joint experts may request directions from the court – see Section 11 above.

17.14 Single joint experts should serve their reports simultaneously on all instructing parties. They should provide a single report even though they may have received instructions which contain areas

---

[1] *Peet v Mid Kent Area Healthcare NHS Trust* [2002] 1 WLR 210.

of conflicting fact or allegation. If conflicting instructions lead to different opinions (for example, because the instructions require experts to make different assumptions of fact), reports may need to contain more than one set of opinions on any issue. It is for the court to determine the facts.

## Cross-examination

17.15 Single joint experts do not normally give oral evidence at trial but if they do, all parties may cross-examine them. In general written questions (CPR 35.6) should be put to single joint experts before requests are made for them to attend court for the purpose of cross-examination.[1]

## Discussions between Experts

18.1 The court has powers to direct discussions between experts for the purposes set out in the Rules (CPR 35.12). Parties may also agree that discussions take place between their experts.

18.2 Where single joint experts have been instructed but parties have, with the permission of the court, instructed their own additional Part 35 experts, there may, if the court so orders or the parties agree, be discussions between the single joint experts and the additional Part 35 experts. Such discussions should be confined to those matters within the remit of the additional Part 35 experts or as ordered by the court.

18.3 The purpose of discussions between experts should be, wherever possible, to:

a. identify and discuss the expert issues in the proceedings;

b. reach agreed opinions on those issues, and, if that is not possible, to narrow the issues in the case;

---

[1] *Daniels v Walker* [2000] 1 WLR 1382.

    c.  identify those issues on which they agree and disagree and summarise their reasons for disagreement on any issue; and

    d.  identify what action, if any, may be taken to resolve any of the outstanding issues between the parties.

*Arrangements for discussions between experts*

18.4    Arrangements for discussions between experts should be proportionate to the value of cases. In small claims and fast track cases there should not normally be meetings between experts. Where discussion is justified in such cases, telephone discussion or an exchange of letters should, in the interests of proportionality, usually suffice. In multi-track cases, discussion may be face to face, but the practicalities or the proportionality principle may require discussions to be by telephone or video conference.

18.5    The parties, their lawyers and experts should co-operate to produce the agenda for any discussion between experts, although primary responsibility for preparation of the agenda should normally lie with the parties' solicitors.

18.6    The agenda should indicate what matters have been agreed and summarise concisely those which are in issue. It is often helpful for it to include questions to be answered by the experts. If agreement cannot be reached promptly or a party is unrepresented, the court may give directions for the drawing up of the agenda. The agenda should be circulated to experts and those instructing them to allow sufficient time for the experts to prepare for the discussion.

18.7    Those instructing experts must not instruct experts to avoid reaching agreement (or to defer doing so) on any matter within the experts' competence. Experts are not permitted to accept such instructions.

18.8   The parties' lawyers may only be present at discussions between experts if all the parties agree or the court so orders. If lawyers do attend, they should not normally intervene except to answer questions put to them by the experts or to advise about the law.[1]

18.9   The content of discussions between experts should not be referred to at trial unless the parties agree (CPR 35.12(4)). It is good practice for any such agreement to be in writing.

18.10  At the conclusion of any discussion between experts, a statement should be prepared setting out:

   a.  a list of issues that have been agreed, including, in each instance, the basis of agreement;

   b.  a list of issues that have not been agreed, including, in each instance, the basis of disagreement;

   c.  a list of any further issues that have arisen that were not included in the original agenda for discussion;

   d.  a record of further action, if any, to be taken or recommended, including as appropriate the holding of further discussions between experts.

18.11  The statement should be agreed and signed by all the parties to the discussion as soon as may be practicable.

18.12  Agreements between experts during discussions do not bind the parties unless the parties expressly agree to be bound by the agreement (CPR 35.12(5)). However, in view of the overriding objective, parties should give careful consideration before refusing to be bound by such an agreement and be able to explain their refusal should it become relevant to the issue of costs.

---

[1]   *Hubbard v Lambeth, Southwark and Lewisham HA* [2001] EWCA 1455.

## Attendance of Experts at Court

19.1 Experts instructed in cases have an obligation to attend court if called upon to do so and accordingly should ensure that those instructing them are always aware of their dates to be avoided and take all reasonable steps to be available.

19.2 Those instructing experts should:

a. ascertain the availability of experts before trial dates are fixed;

b. keep experts updated with timetables (including the dates and times experts are to attend) and the location of the court;

c. give consideration, where appropriate, to experts giving evidence via a video-link.

d. inform experts immediately if trial dates are vacated.

19.3 Experts should normally attend court without the need for the service of witness summonses, but on occasion they may be served to require attendance (CPR 34). The use of witness summonses does not affect the contractual or other obligations of the parties to pay experts' fees.

# CRIMINAL PROCEDURE RULES PART 24 – DISCLOSURE OF EXPERT EVIDENCE

*Requirement to disclose expert evidence*

24.1   1. Following –

   a. A plea of not guilty by any person to an alleged offence in respect of which a magistrates' court proceeds to summary trial;

   b. the committal for trial of any person;

   c. the transfer to the Crown Court of any proceedings for the trial of a person by virtue of a notice of transfer given under section 4 of the Criminal Justice Act 1987;[1]

   d. the transfer to the Crown Court of any proceedings for the trial of a person by virtue of a notice of transfer served on a magistrates' court under section 53 of the Criminal Justice Act 1991;[2]

---

[1]   1987 c. 38; section 4 was amended by the Criminal Justice Act 1988 (c.33), section 144(1) and (2), the Legal Aid Act 1988 (c.34), Schedule 5, paragraph 22, the Criminal Justice and Public Order Act 1994 (c.33), Schedule 9, paragraph 29, the Crime and Disorder Act 1998 (c.37), Schedule 8, paragraph 65 and the Access to Justice Act 1999 (c.22), Schedule 4, paragraphs 38 and 39. Section 4 is repealed by the Criminal Justice Act 2003 (c.44), section 41 and Schedule 3, Part 2, paragraph 58(1), (2) and Schedule 37, Part 4, with effect from a date to be appointed.

[2]   1991 c. 53; section 53 was amended by the Criminal Justice and Public Order Act 1994 (c.33), Schedule 9, paragraph 49, the Crime and Disorder Act 1998 (c.37), Schedule 8, paragraph 93 and the Access to Justice Act 1999 (c.22), Schedule 4, paragraph 47. Section 53 is repealed by the Criminal Justice Act 2003 (c.44), Schedule 37, Part 4, with effect from a date to be appointed.

e. the sending of any person for trial under section 51 of the Crime and Disorder Act 1998;[1]

f. the preferring of a bill of indictment charging a person with an offence under the authority of section 2(2)(b) of the Administration of Justice (Miscellaneous Provisions) Act 1933;[2] or

g. the making of an order for the retrial of any person,

if any party to the proceedings proposes to adduce expert evidence (whether of fact or opinion) in the proceedings (otherwise than in relation to sentence) he shall as soon as practicable, unless in relation to the evidence in question he has already done so or the evidence is the subject of an application for leave to adduce such evidence in accordance with section 41 of the Youth Justice and Criminal Evidence Act 1999 –[3]

i. furnish the other party or parties and the court with a statement in writing of any finding or opinion which he proposes to adduce by way of such evidence, and notify the expert of this disclosure, and

ii. where a request in writing is made to him in that behalf by any other party, provide that party also with a copy of (or if it appears to the party proposing to adduce the evidence to be more practicable, a reasonable opportunity to examine) the record of any observation, test, calculation or other procedure on which such

---

[1]  1998 c. 37; section 51 is substituted by new sections 51 and 51A to 51E by the Criminal Justice Act 2003 (c.44), Schedule 3, Part 1, paragraphs 15 and 18, with effect from a date to be appointed.

[2]  1933 c. 36; section 2(2)(b) was amended by the Criminal Appeal Act 1964 (c.43), Schedule 2, the Supreme Court Act 1981 (c.54), Schedule 5 and the Prosecution of Offences Act 1985 (c.23), Schedule 2.

[3]  1999 c. 23.

finding or opinion is based and any document or other thing or substance in respect of which any such procedure has been carried out.

2.  A party may by notice in writing waive his right to be furnished with any of the matters mentioned in paragraph (1) and, in particular, may agree that the statement mentioned in paragraph (1)(a) may be furnished to him orally and not in writing.

3.  In paragraph (1), "document" means anything in which information of any description is recorded.

Formerly rule 3 of the Magistrates' Courts (Advance Notice of Expert Evidence) Rules 1997[1] and rule 3 of the Crown Court (Advance Notice of Expert Evidence) Rules 1987.[2] For the equivalent requirement in Crown Court proceedings under Part 2 of the Proceeds of Crime Act 2002 see rule 57.9. Part 33 contains rules about the duties of an expert and the content of an expert's report.

*Withholding evidence*

24.2  1.  If a party has reasonable grounds for believing that the disclosure of any evidence in compliance with the requirements imposed by rule 24.1 might lead to the intimidation, or attempted intimidation, of any person on whose evidence he intends to rely in the proceedings, or otherwise to the course of justice being interfered with, he shall not be obliged to comply with those requirements in relation to that evidence.

2.  Where, in accordance with paragraph (1), a party considers that he is not obliged to comply with the requirements

---

[1]   S.I. 1997/705.

[2]   S.I. 1987/716; amended by S.I. 1997/700 and S.I. 2000/2987.

imposed by rule 24.1 with regard to any evidence in relation to any other party, he shall give notice in writing to that party to the effect that the evidence is being withheld and the grounds for doing so.

Formerly rule 4 of the Magistrates' Courts (Advance Notice of Expert Evidence) Rules 1997 and rule 4 of the Crown Court (Advance Notice of Expert Evidence) Rules 1987. For the equivalent exception in Crown Court proceedings under Part 2 of the Proceeds of Crime Act 2002 see rule 57.10.

*Effect of failure to disclose*

24.3    A party who seeks to adduce expert evidence in any proceedings and who fails to comply with rule 24.1 shall not adduce that evidence in those proceedings without the leave of the court.

Formerly rule 5 of the Magistrates' Courts (Advance Notice of Expert Evidence) Rules 1997 and rule 5 of the Crown Court (Advance Notice of Expert Evidence) Rules 1987.

# CRIMINAL PROCEDURE RULES
# PART 33 – EXPERT EVIDENCE

*[Note. See rule 2.1(4) for the application of the rules in this Part. Part 24 contains rules about the disclosure of the substance of expert evidence. For the use of an expert report as evidence, see section 30 of the Criminal Justice Act 1988.][1]*

*Reference to expert*

33.1 A reference to an 'expert' in this Part is a reference to a person who is required to give or prepare expert evidence for the purpose of criminal proceedings, including evidence required to determine fitness to plead or for the purpose of sentencing.

*[Note. Expert medical evidence may be required to determine fitness to plead under section 4 of the Criminal Procedure (Insanity) Act 1964.[2] It may be required also under section 11 of the Powers of Criminal Courts (Sentencing) Act 2000,[3] under Part III of the Mental Health Act 1983[4] or under Part 12 of the Criminal Justice Act 2003.[5] Those Acts contain requirements about the qualification of medical experts.]*

---

[1]  1988 c. 33, section 30(4A), was inserted by section 47 of, and paragraph 32 of Schedule 1 to, the Criminal Procedure and Investigations Act 1996 (c. 25) and is repealed by section 41 to, and paragraph 60(1) and (6) of Schedule 3 and Schedule 37 to, the Criminal Justice Act 2003, with effect from a date to be appointed.

[2]  1964 c. 84; section 4 was amended by section 2 of the Criminal Procedure (Insanity and Unfitness to Plead) Act 1991 (c. 25) and section 22(1),(2) and (3) of the Domestic Violence, Crime and Victims Act 2004 (c. 28).

[3]  2000 c. 6.

[4]  1983 c. 20 .

[5]  2003 c. 44.

*Expert's duty to the court*

33.2  1.  An expert must help the court to achieve the overriding objective by giving objective, unbiased opinion on matters within his expertise.

2. This duty overrides any obligation to the person from whom he receives instructions or by whom he is paid.

3. This duty includes an obligation to inform all parties and the court if the expert's opinion changes from that contained in a report served as evidence or given in a statement under Part 24 or Part 29.

*Content of expert's report*

33.3  1.  An expert's report must –

a. give details of the expert's qualifications, relevant experience and accreditation;

b. give details of any literature or other information which the expert has relied on in making the report;

c. contain a statement setting out the substance of all facts given to the expert which are material to the opinions expressed in the report or upon which those opinions are based;

d. make clear which of the facts stated in the report are within the expert's own knowledge;

e. say who carried out any examination, measurement, test or experiment which the expert has used for the report and –

   i. give the qualifications, relevant experience and accreditation of that person,

ii. say whether or not the examination, measurement, test or experiment was carried out under the expert's supervision, and

iii. summarise the findings on which the expert relies;

f. where there is a range of opinion on the matters dealt with in the report –

i. summarise the range of opinion, and

ii. give reasons for his own opinion;

g. if the expert is not able to give his opinion without qualification, state the qualification;

h. contain a summary of the conclusions reached;

i. contain a statement that the expert understands his duty to the court, and has complied and will continue to comply with that duty; and

j. contain the same declaration of truth as a witness statement.

2. Only sub-paragraphs (i) and (j) of rule 33.3(1) apply to a summary by an expert of his conclusions served in advance of that expert's report.

*[Note. Part 24 contains rules about the disclosure of the substance of expert evidence. Part 27 contains rules about witness statements. Declarations of truth in witness statements are required by section 9 of the Criminal Justice Act 1967[1] and section 5B of the Magistrates' Courts*

---

[1]   1967 c. 80; section 9 is amended by section 72(3) of, and paragraph 55 of Schedule 5 to, the Children and Young Persons Act 1969 (c. 54) and sections 41 and 332 of, and paragraph 43(1) and (2) of Schedule 3 and Schedule 37 to, the Criminal Justice Act 2003 (c. 44), with effect from dates to be appointed.

*Act 1980.[1] A party who accepts another party's expert's conclusions may admit them as facts under section 10 of the Criminal Justice Act 1967.[2] Evidence of examinations, etc. on which an expert relies may be admissible under section 127 of the Criminal Justice Act 2003.][3]*

*Expert to be informed of service of report*

33.4 A party who serves on another party or on the court a report by an expert must, at once, inform that expert of that fact.

*Pre-hearing discussion of expert evidence*

33.5 1. This rule applies where more than one party wants to introduce expert evidence.

2. The court may direct the experts to –

   a. discuss the expert issues in the proceedings; and

   b. prepare a statement for the court of the matters on which they agree and disagree, giving their reasons.

3. Except for that statement, the content of that discussion must not be referred to without the court's permission.

*Failure to comply with directions*

33.6 A party may not introduce expert evidence without the court's permission if the expert has not complied with a direction under rule 33.5.

---

[1] 1980 c. 43; section 5B was inserted by section 47 of, and paragraph 3 of Schedule 1 to, the Criminal Procedure and Investigations Act 1996 (c. 25) and is amended by section 72(3) of, and paragraph 55 of Schedule 5 to, the Children and Young Persons Act 1969 (c. 54), with effect from a date to be appointed. It is repealed by sections 41 and 332 of, and paragraph 51(1) and (3) of Schedule 3 and Schedule 37 to, the Criminal Justice Act 2003 (c.44), with effect from a date to be appointed.

[2] 1967 c. 80.

[3] 2003 c. 44; section 127 was amended by article 3 of, and paragraphs 45 and 50 of the Schedule to, S.I. 2004/2035..

*[Note. At a pre-trial hearing a court may make binding rulings about the admissibility of evidence and about questions of law under section 7 of the Criminal Justice Act 1987;[1] sections 31 and 40 of the Criminal Procedure and Investigations Act 1996;[2] and section 45 of the Courts Act 2003.][3]*

### Court's power to direct that evidence is to be given by a single joint expert

33.7   1.   Where more than one defendant wants to introduce expert evidence on an issue at trial, the court may direct that the evidence on that issue is to be given by one expert only.

2.   Where the co-defendants cannot agree who should be the expert, the court may –

a.   select the expert from a list prepared or identified by them; or

b.   direct that the expert be selected in such other manner as the court may direct.

### Instructions to a single joint expert

33.8   1.   Where the court gives a direction under rule 33.7 for a single joint expert to be used, each of the co-defendants may give instructions to the expert.

---

[1]   1987 c. 38; section 7 was amended by section 168(1) of, and paragraph 30 of Schedule 9 to, the Criminal Justice and Public Order Act 1994 (c. 33) and section 310(1) of the Criminal Justice Act 2003 (c. 44) and is further amended by sections 45 and 331 of, and paragraphs 52 and 53 of Schedule 36 to, the Criminal Justice Act 2003 (c. 44), with effect from dates to be appointed. Section 7(3),(4) and (5) was repealed by sections 72 and 80 of, and paragraph 2 of Schedule 3 and Schedule 5 to, the Criminal Procedure and Investigations Act 1996 (c. 25).

[2]   1996 c. 25; section 31 is amended by sections 310(5), 331 and 332 of, and paragraphs 20, 36, 65 and 67 of Schedule 36 and Schedule 37 to, the Criminal Justice Act 2003 (c. 44), with effect from dates to be appointed.

[3]   2003 c. 39.

2. When a co-defendant gives instructions to the expert he must, at the same time, send a copy of the instructions to the other co-defendant(s).

3. The court may give directions about –

   a. the payment of the expert's fees and expenses; and

   b. any examination, measurement, test or experiment which the expert wishes to carry out.

4. The court may, before an expert is instructed, limit the amount that can be paid by way of fees and expenses to the expert.

5. Unless the court otherwise directs, the instructing co-defendants are jointly and severally liable for the payment of the expert's fees and expenses.

# FAMILY PROCEDURE (ADOPTION) RULES – PART 17

*Duty to restrict expert evidence*

154 Expert evidence shall be restricted to that which is reasonably required to resolve the proceedings.

*Interpretation*

155 A reference to an 'expert' in this Part –

a. is a reference to an expert who has been instructed to give or prepare evidence for the purpose of court proceedings; and

b. does not include –

i. a person who is within a prescribed description for the purposes of section 94(1) of the Act (persons who may prepare a report for any person about the suitability of a child for adoption or of a person to adopt a child or about the adoption, or placement for adoption, of a child); or

ii. an officer of the Service or a Welsh family proceedings officer when acting in that capacity.

(Regulation 3 of the Restriction on the Preparation of Adoption Reports Regulations 2005 (S.I. 2005/1711) sets out which persons are within a prescribed description for the purposes of section 94(1) of the Act.)

*Experts' overriding duty to the court*

156 1. It is the duty of an expert to help the court on the matters within his expertise.

2. This duty overrides any obligation to the person from whom he has received instructions or by whom he is paid.

*Court's power to restrict expert evidence*

157   1. No party may call an expert or put in evidence an expert's report without the court's permission.

2. When a party applies for permission under this rule he must identify –

   a. the field in which he wishes to rely on expert evidence; and

   b. where practicable the expert in that field on whose evidence he wishes to rely.

3. If permission is granted under this rule it shall be in relation only to the expert named or the field identified under paragraph (2).

4. The court may limit the amount of the expert's fees and expenses that the party who wishes to rely on the expert may recover from any other party.

*General requirement for expert evidence to be given in a written report*

158   Expert evidence is to be given in a written report unless the court directs otherwise.

*Written questions to experts*

159   1. A party may put to –

   a. an expert instructed by another party; or

   b. a single joint expert appointed under rule 160,

   written questions about his report.

2. Written questions under paragraph (1) –

   a. may be put once only;

   b. must be put within 5 days beginning with the date on which the expert's report was served; and

   c. must be for the purpose only of clarification of the report,

   unless in any case –

   i. the court gives permission;

   ii. the other party agrees; or

   iii. any practice direction provides otherwise.

3. An expert's answers to questions put in accordance with paragraph (1) shall be treated as part of the expert's report.

4. Where –

   a. a party has put a written question to an expert instructed by another party in accordance with this rule; and

   b. the expert does not answer that question,

   the court may make one or both of the following orders in relation to the party who instructed the expert –

   i. that the party may not rely on the evidence of that expert; or

   ii. that the party may not recover the fees and expenses of that expert from any other party.

*Court's power to direct that evidence is to be given by a single joint expert*

160   1.  Where two or more parties wish to submit expert evidence on a particular issue, the court may direct that the evidence on that issue is to given by one expert only.

       2.  The parties wishing to submit the expert evidence are called 'the instructing parties'.

       3.  Where the instructing parties cannot agree who should be the expert, the court may –

          a.  select the expert from a list prepared or identified by the instructing parties; or

          b.  direct that the expert be selected in such other manner as the court may direct.

*Instructions to a single joint expert*

161   1.  Where the court gives a direction under rule 160 for a single joint expert to be used, each instructing party may give instructions to the expert.

       2.  When an instructing party gives instructions to the expert he must, at the same time, send a copy of the instructions to the other instructing parties.

       3.  The court may give directions about –

          a.  the payment of the expert's fees and expenses; and

          b.  any inspection, examination or experiments which the expert wishes to carry out.

4. The court may, before an expert is instructed, limit the amount that can be paid by way of fees and expenses to the expert.

5. Unless the court otherwise directs, the instructing parties are jointly and severally liable for the payment of the expert's fees and expenses.

*Power of court to direct a party to provide information*

162   1. Where a party has access to information which is not reasonably available to the other party, the court may direct the party who has access to the information to prepare and file a document recording the information.

2. A court officer will send a copy of that document to the other party.

*Contents of report*

163   1. An expert's report must comply with the requirements set out in the relevant practice direction.

2. At the end of an expert's report there must be a statement that –

a. the expert understands his duty to the court; and

b. he has complied with that duty.

3. The expert's report must state the substance of all material instructions, whether written or oral, on the basis of which the report was written.

4. The instructions referred to in paragraph (3) shall not be privileged against disclosure.

*Use by one party of expert's report disclosed by another*

164     Where a party has disclosed an expert's report, any party may use that expert's report as evidence at the final hearing.

*Discussions between experts*

165     1.  The court may, at any stage, direct a discussion between experts for the purpose of requiring the experts to –

   a.  identify and discuss the expert issues in the proceedings; and

   b.  where possible, reach an agreed opinion on those issues.

   2.  The court may specify the issues which the experts must discuss.

   3.  The court may direct that following a discussion between the experts they must prepare a statement for the court showing –

   a.  those issues on which they agree; and

   b.  those issues on which they disagree and a summary of their reasons for disagreeing.

*Consequence of failure to disclose expert's report*

166     A party who fails to disclose an expert's report may not use the report at the final hearing or call the expert to give evidence orally unless the court gives permission.

*Expert's right to ask court for directions*

167     1.  An expert may file a written request for directions to assist him in carrying out his function as an expert.

2.  An expert must, unless the court directs otherwise, provide a copy of any proposed request for directions under paragraph (1) –

    a.  to the party instructing him, at least 7 days before he files the request; and

    b.  to all other parties, at least 4 days before he files it.

3.  The court, when it gives directions, may also direct that a party be served with a copy of the directions.

# GLOSSARY
## of some common legal terms

**Action**
Civil legal proceedings.

**Admissible evidence**
Evidence that is permitted to be heard or read in court and taken into account.

**Adversarial system**
The method of deciding cases in court whereby the opposing parties argue their standpoints.

**Advocate**
A lawyer who pleads the case of his/her client. This may be a barrister or increasingly a solicitor. (A witness is not an advocate.)

**Affirmation**
A non-religious alternative to the oath but of equal weight. A witness lying after affirming in court is liable to be charged with perjury.

**Alternative dispute resolution (ADR)**
A collective term for a number of different ways of settling a dispute other than by litigation, e.g. mediation.

**Appeal**
Proceedings taken in a higher court to overturn a lower court's decision in a case on the grounds that it was erroneously made or incorrect in law.

**Arbitration**
An adjudication process operating outside the court structure. The decision of the arbitrator is legally binding. Arbitration may be ordered by the court or agreed to by the parties.

**Assessment**
A procedure, previously known as taxation, by which the court decides the amount of legal costs to be paid at the end of an action.

**Assessor**
An expert appointed by the court to assist the judge in some civil cases.

**Barrister**
A qualified lawyer who is a member of one of the four Inns of Court and has been called to the bar. Barristers can work in all courts and are instructed by solicitors, not members of the public. They are self-employed, work from offices called chambers and wear wigs and gowns in court (other than in the Magistrates' Court).

**Bar vocational course**
A one year academic and practical course with exams at the end which enables a person to qualify as a barrister. This is undertaken by law graduates or non-law graduates who have passed the Common Professional Exam. A further one year's pupillage (training with a senior barrister) is necessary before they can work as self-employed barristers.

**Brief**
The document summarising a case that is prepared by a solicitor and sent to the advocate in order that he/she may advise on the case and, if necessary, subsequently appear in court.

**Burden and standard of proof**
Having the burden of proof means that party must be the one to prove their case. The standard of proof is the level of proof that must be demonstrated by a party for the court to rule in their favour. In civil cases this level is "on the balance of probabilities", while in criminal cases it is "beyond reasonable doubt".

**Case**
A particular legal claim.

**Case management**
Decisions or actions taken by the court to progress a civil action.

**Causation**
The relationship between cause and effect.

**Civil case**
A dispute between two parties in which one seeks redress from the other.

**Civil Procedure Rules 1998**
The new rules of court for civil claims brought into effect in April 1999 following Lord Woolf's *Access to Justice* inquiry.

**Claimant**
A person who makes a legal claim, previously a plaintiff.

**Claim form**

The document which starts a civil action, previously a writ or summons.

**Client**

A member of the public, business or organisation who instructs a solicitor to act on their behalf.

**Common Professional Exam (CPE)**

An exam taken by non-law graduates at the end of an intensive year studying law. It is the first stage in training to become a solicitor or barrister.

**Compensation**

Payment to an injured party as redress for the injury, damage or loss suffered.

**Conduct money**

The money repaid to a witness of fact for the cost of transport from home to court, plus a fee and any loss of pay.

**Conference**

A meeting between an advocate and the solicitor, client and/or expert.

**Contemporaneous note**

A record or note made by a witness at the time of the event happening or shortly afterwards while it was still fresh in the mind.

**Counsel**

A barrister.

**Counterclaim**

A claim by the defendant in a civil case that the claimant has caused the defendant a loss or damages, rather than the other way round.

**County Court**

A civil court where the lower value claims for damages by a claimant are managed and decided.

**Court bundle**

The documents most relevant to the case to be tried in court. They are ordered and numbered and are available for witnesses to look at in court.

**Criminal case**

A case brought on behalf of the State against an individual who has broken the criminal law.

**Cross-examination**

The questioning of a witness by the party who did not call them, with the object of testing their evidence.

**Crown Court**

A criminal court with a judge and jury. The jury decides if the defendant is guilty or not guilty. The most serious criminal offences are heard in the Crown Court.

**Crown Prosecution Service (CPS)**

The organisation that brings prosecutions on behalf of the State.

**Damages**

Money paid as compensation.

**Decision**

The judgment of the court.

**Defendant**

In civil trials: the person sued. In criminal trials: the person accused of a crime.

**Disclosure**

The showing of each party's documentary evidence to the other before a trial.

**Either way offences**

Criminal offences which may be tried either in the Crown Court or the Magistrates' Court.

**Evidence**

The means by which something is proved. Written evidence may comprise statements, reports or other documents. Oral evidence is the spoken evidence of witnesses in court.

**Examination in chief**

The first questions asked of a witness in court by the lawyer representing the party who has asked that witness to give evidence.

**Expert**

Non-lawyer specialist in a particular field who is asked by client/solicitor to give an independent opinion on aspects of a case. Their role in court as a witness is to help the decision-maker(s) (judge/jury/magistrates) to understand and decide the case.

**Fast Track**

One of the new civil case management tracks, mainly for claims of £5,000-£15,000.

**Hearsay**

What someone has overheard or been told happened rather than what they saw happen themselves. Hearsay evidence, being "second-hand", is inadmissible in criminal trials.

**High Court**

A civil court where the higher value claims are heard.

**Indictable only**

A criminal offence which is of a serious nature and the trial of which must take place in the Crown Court.

**Indictment**

The document which sets out the charge against a defendant in serious offences.

**Injury**

Physical injury, loss or damage.

**Inspection**

The looking at documents of the opposing party prior to the trial.

**Issue of proceedings**

The formal process by which a claimant starts litigation in the court system.

**Judgment**

The decision or sentence of the court.

**Jury**

Twelve members of the public who decide whether a defendant in a criminal trial is guilty or not based on the evidence presented in court. Juries are also used in a limited number of civil cases to decide between the parties.

**Lawyer**

A barrister or solicitor.

**Legal aid**

Taxpayers' money available to help to pay the costs of court cases for those of limited means.

### Legal Practice Course (LPC)
A one year course of academic and practical study, with exams, taken by law graduates or those who are non-law graduates but who have passed the Common Professional Exam. Passing the LPC is the first stage in becoming a solicitor. A further two years' training at a solicitors firm is necessary before the person becomes a solicitor.

### Letter before action/Letter of claim
A letter sent by the claimant's solicitor to the defendant setting out the claimant's case and inviting the defendant to settle the matter.

### Liability
The responsibility for an action or an event that results in loss or damage.

### Magistrate
A lay Justice of the Peace who sits with one or two others to try cases in the Magistrates' Court. A stipendiary magistrate is a legally qualified paid Justice who sits alone.

### Magistrates' Court
The lowest criminal court. All cases start here and, depending on their seriousness, are either tried by the magistrates or sent to a higher court. Decisions as to bail are also made. Other responsibilities of Magistrates' Courts include licensing and family matters.

### Multi Track
One of the new civil case management tracks, mainly for claims over £15,000.

### Negligence
A failure of duty of care that results in loss or injury.

### Oath
A formal religious declaration made by a witness before they give their evidence to say that they will tell the truth. If a witness lies having taken an oath in court, they may be charged with perjury. An oath carries the same weight as an affirmation.

### Offer to settle
Formal offer to settle a civil claim, with costs consequences, which can be made by a claimant or defendant at any stage, including before proceedings are started.

**Opinion evidence**
The view of an independent expert in a specialist field on the facts of a case.

**Particulars of claim**
A formal document produced by the claimant in a civil case setting out the details of their case and what they want if they win.

**Party**
One of the "sides" in a case, i.e. the claimant or the defendant. There may also be a third party involved.

**Payment into court**
A sum of money paid to the court by a defendant as an offer to settle a civil case. If accepted by the claimant, the case ends. If not accepted and the claimant wins but is awarded a lower sum in damages, the claimant becomes liable for all the legal costs of the case.

**Pre-action protocol**
Best practice guidance about steps which should be taken before proceedings are issued in civil claims.

**Privilege**
The protection from general public knowledge of a document, statement or report, which was prepared for the purpose of litigation.

**Professional witness**
A witness who gives evidence as a result of seeing or doing something in the course of their everyday job; for example, police officers or police surgeons. These witnesses give mainly factual evidence, but can give opinion evidence in areas within their specialist field of knowledge.

**Prosecution**
The bringing of a criminal case against a defendant. A prosecution is usually brought on behalf of the State by the Crown Prosecution Service but may be brought by a private individual or body in the form of a private prosecution.

**Quantum**
Amount (of money by way of compensation/damages).

**Queen's Counsel (QC)**
A senior barrister who usually has 20 or more years' experience. Sometimes known as a "silk" or "leading counsel".

## Re-examination

The third set of questions asked of a witness in court by the lawyer representing the party who has asked that witness to give evidence. It follows the examination in chief and the cross-examination. The intention is to allow the witness to comment further on issues arising from the cross-examination.

## Section 9 statement (Criminal Justice Act 1967)

A witness statement that is accepted by the opposing party. This lack of objection allows the statement to be read in court without the need for the witness to give oral evidence and be cross-examined.

## Settlement

An agreement between the parties to end a case without going to trial.

## Single or joint expert

One expert instructed by the parties jointly, rather than each party instructing their own expert.

## Silk

Queen's Counsel, a senior barrister.

## Solicitor

A qualified lawyer who may be instructed directly by members of the public. All solicitors may appear as advocates in certain courts but only those with particular experience or qualifications may appear in the higher courts. They are either self-employed or work in partnerships (called practices).

## Statement of case

A formal court document that each party produces in a civil claim setting out their case.

## Summary judgment

Judgment without a full trial in a civil claim.

## Summary only offence

A criminal offence of a minor nature that can be tried only in the Magistrates' Court.

## Summary trial

A criminal trial which takes place in the Magistrates' Court.

**Terms and conditions**
The details of the contract between an expert and the client/solicitor who has instructed him/her, including when and how the expert is to be paid.

**Trial**
A court hearing to decide whether or not a defendant is guilty in a criminal case or which party wins in a civil case.

**Vicarious liability**
The legal liability of a person or organisation for the acts of another, e.g. a health authority may be liable for the work done by a doctor employed by them.

**Without prejudice**
Without prejudging an issue. Without prejudice negotiations may take place between parties which, if unsuccessful, will not have a bearing on the court case as anything discussed will be inadmissible in court.

**Witness of fact**
A person who has seen or heard something themselves and gives evidence in court.

**Witness summons**
A written order by the court demanding the attendance of a witness at court. Non attendance will be contempt of court and may result in imprisonment.